THE GOSPEL OF THE UNKNOWN JESUS

THE SECRET TEACHINGS OF JESUS FROM THE APOCRYPHAL AND GNOSTIC GOSPELS

Edited and with Introduction by

RICHARD J. HOOPER

SANCTUARY PUBLICATIONS

The Gospel of the Unknown Jesus: The Teachings of Jesus from the Apocryphal and Gnostic Gospels

Original painting of Jesus by Susan Lovit
Cover and book design by Jane Perini, Thunder Mountain Design and Communications
Photography by Sharon Hooper

ISBN 0-9746995-5-1
Library of Congress Control Number 2006923935

Excerpts from *The Nag Hammadi Library* in English, 3rd COMPLETELY REVISED EDITION by James M. Robinson, General Editor.
Copyright © 1978, 1988 by E.J. Brill, Leiden, The Netherlands.
Reprinted by permission of HarperCollins Publishers.

Table of Contents

Selections from:

The Gospel of Thomas,
The Gospel of the Savior,
The Gospel of Mary,
The Gospel of Eve
The Gospel of Philip
The Gospel of the Nazareans
The Gospel of the Egyptians
The Gospel of the Hebrews
The Gospel of the Ebionites
The Living Gospel of Mani
The Gospel of Truth
The Book of the Great Logos
The Book of Thomas the Contender
The Book of John the Evangelist
The Book of Mysteries
The Book of the Great Logos
The Apocryphon of James
The Apocryphon of John
The First Apocalypse of James
The Second Apocalypse of James
The Coptic-Gnostic Apocalypse of Peter
The Epistula Apostolorum
Dialogue of the Savior
The Sophia of Jesus Christ
The Acts of John

The Pistis Sophia
Codex Bezae
The Coptic Psalter
The Two Books of Jeu
The Kerygmata Petrou
The Naassene Psalm of the Soul
The Mandaean Liturgy
The Second Treatise of the Great Seth

Introduction

THE HISTORICAL JESUS

To his disciples—those who actually walked and talked with him—Jesus was a wisdom teacher and religious reformer in the tradition of Israel's great prophets. But he was much more than this to them. His closest disciples perceived him as someone who had exceptional insight into the nature of reality and the purpose of human existence. But what attracted them to him in the first place was their recognition that he actually lived what he taught.

While the disciples saw Jesus as a mystic and a holy man, they did not—contrary to orthodox Christian dogma—believe that he was the Messiah or the son of God.[1] In fact, the historical Jesus discouraged such thinking. These specific Christian beliefs belong to second and third generation followers who were attempting to make theological sense out of Jesus' untimely and horrific death. Unfortunately, in the process of transforming a Jewish holy man into a world savior, Christians traded the religion *of* Jesus for a religion *about* him.

Also contrary to popular Christian opinion, Jesus was not an apocalyptic preacher; he did not believe that the end of the world was imminent.[2] Although the authors of the canonical Gospels portrayed him as an apocalyptic prophet in the mold of John the Baptist, the historical Jesus seems to have been entirely disinterested in a coming apocalypse.

To the contrary; Jesus believed that the Kingdom of God was not some future cosmic event, but a present reality—an inner state of mind. He taught others that those who had true spiritual perception could recognize the Kingdom all around them, and most especially, within themselves. The Kingdom, according to Jesus, is not a place or a time, it is a state of Being in the human heart. When one is completely absorbed in God, there is no place where the Kingdom is not.

Because they were the products of later Christians—and not written by Jesus' actual followers—the canonical Gospels are not historical reports, but statements of faith which were written to encourage the faithful and win over the non-believer.[3] The anonymous Christian evangelists who wrote the Gospels were not historians, nor did they intend to be. In the ancient world, mythology was often seen as more true and more real than mere historical fact. It was the meaning of historical events that was important.

To the evangelists, if Jesus didn't literally rise the dead and turn water into wine, that was irrelevant. He was a god/man, so he certainly could have done those things if he had wanted to.

Evangelical Christians, as well as Christian fundamentalists will, of course, reject virtually everything I have just written, but *New Testament* scholars in mainline Christian denominations have known for more than a century that most of the words attributed to Jesus in the Gospels were the inventions of Christian evangelists, and that most stories about what Jesus did were myths, not historical reports.[4] All of this was already old news when I entered seminary more than three decades ago, although it was certainly news—and very shocking news—to us seminarians at the time.

While it is not the purpose of this present work to debate the many issues surrounding the modern quest for the historical Jesus, I do need to give some justification here for making the statements above. And for this, we must turn the clock back to the first and second centuries of the Common Era.

The first narrative Gospel, *The Gospel According to Mark*, was written no earlier than 70 C.E., and the last narrative Gospel, *The Gospel According to Luke*, may have been written as late as 120 C.E.[5] But before there were narrative Gospels, there were "source" Gospels, and before that—oral tradition.

At least three "source" Gospels have been identified by modern scholars. Here we will deal with just two of these. As "source Gospels", they include no stories about Jesus, but are simply collections of his teachings.

The source documents also tell us a great deal about Jesus' earliest followers. They show us what these men and women believed about Jesus. The Jesus of these collections was the only Jesus they knew.

The two source Gospels in question were written at least twenty years before Mark wrote the first narrative Gospel, so it is likely that the teachings of Jesus in these texts were based on the oral traditions of Jesus' earliest disciples. As a consequence, these two Gospels represent the closest thing we have to the actual testimony of Jesus' original disciples.

One of these collections of Jesus' sayings, or logia, is *The Gospel According to Thomas*. The other work is known as *The Gospel of Q* (the letter "Q" being the first letter of the German word, "quell", meaning "source"), which is also known as the "Synoptic Sayings Source".[6]

Although a few fragments of *The Gospel of Thomas*, written in Greek, were discovered at Oxyrhynchus in Egypt during the nineteenth century, a complete manuscript of *Thomas* was discovered at Nag Hammadi, Egypt, in 1945. This text was discovered sealed in an earthenware jar which had been buried in the hot Egyptian soil for more than fifteen centuries.

Thomas is one of fifty-two different "tractates", that were found in thirteen leather-bound codices, or books. All of these long lost sacred scriptures were written by Coptic-Gnostic Christians, and the entire collection is now known as the Nag Hammadi Library.

Unlike *The Gospel of Thomas*, there are no extant copies of the *The Gospel of Q* because scholars first discovered *Q* embedded within the Gospels of *Matthew* and *Luke*. For decades, scholars referred to *Q* as a "hypothetical" gospel, but today nearly all scholars are convinced that *Q* was, in fact, a written gospel at one point, and that it circulated among the earliest Jesus communities after Jesus' death.

The *Gospel of Thomas* consists of two layers of transmission. The earliest layer is dated to 50 C.E., and a later redaction to the end of the first century C. E. *The Gospel of Q* consists of three layers of transmission, and these are designated by scholars as Q^1, Q^2 and Q^3. Q^1, like the earliest layer of Thomas, is thought to have been written around 50 C. E. Q^2 and Q^3 were written sometime later—but probably before 70 C.E.

If Q^1, and the earliest layer of *Thomas*, represent what Jesus' earliest followers believed about him, then orthodox Christian dogma is in trouble. Neither of these earliest of all Gospels show any interest in Jesus as the Messiah, nor do they propose in any way that Jesus was divine.[7] Additionally, the Jesus of *Thomas* and Q^1 does not make apocalyptic pronouncements of any kind.[8] Only in the later layers of Q (Q^2 and Q^3) do we find the first evidence of believers putting apocalyptic statements into the mouth of Jesus.[9]

Most shocking of all, the Jesus people who originally compiled these texts gave no theological meaning to Jesus' death, much less to his "resurrection". The two earliest Gospels have no stories at all about the life or death of Jesus. Jesus' earliest followers seemed to have been interested only in preserving his teachings, and none of those teachings had anything to do with later Christian theology.

Earliest Christianity (or as many scholars refer to it today, the Christ cult) did not emerge out of the Jesus movement. It was an entirely separate movement, and one of its leaders—if not its very founder—was the self-proclaimed apostle of Christ, Paul. Christianity as we know it today was founded on the theology of Paul, not on Jesus or his teachings.

HERETICS AND HIDDEN BOOKS

Belief in Jesus as the Messiah, Savior and son of God were the theological products of Hellenistic Christians who, for the most part, were also gentiles. But Hellenistic Christianity was not a cohesive movement, it was a collection of different faiths that found different expressions in different locations throughout the Roman Empire.[10] While all of these forms of Christianity held some beliefs in common—that Jesus was the Messiah, a world savior and the son of God—they widely disagreed on what these terms actually meant.

Contrary to the claims of the Church throughout history, a single

Christian doctrine did not exist until the fourth century when "orthodox" Christianity became the state religion of Rome under Constantine. "Orthodox" Christianity did not become the only Christianity until Constantine outlawed all other versions of the faith.

Prior to the fourth century, Christianity was an incredibly diverse religion. While many religions begin with a single theology that eventually evolves into different forms, quite the opposite was the case with Christianity. And since so many different forms of Christianity once existed, so did hundreds of different gospels, epistles, apocryphons (hidden books) and apocalypses.

Many early Christian texts had a wide circulation, while others were specific to certain locations and groups of believers. Whatever their specific beliefs, all of these Christians had two things in common: They all believed that they represented the only authentic form of Christianity, and that their scriptures represented the one, true and original Christian doctrine.

Each form of Christianity also traced its origins to the historical Jesus, and each claimed authority to preach and teach in his name. Contrary to the claims of the early Church, many of these widely disparate versions of Christianity came into being at precisely the same moment "orthodox" Christianity did. To this extent, they could all claim to be the "original" form of Christian faith.

We find in the writings of Paul to his churches in Corinth and Galatia, his complaints against "false apostles" who were preaching "false gospels" in his churches whenever he was absent. According to Paul, these wolves in sheep's clothing were having a certain amount of success in stealing his own converts. Many scholars now believe that the "false" apostles Paul describes in his letters to the Corinthians and Galatians were, in fact, Gnostic-Christians.

This being the case, the Church's claim that Gnosticism was a late heresy and perversion of "original" Christian faith is entirely false. In fact, two of the founding fathers of Gnosticism are mentioned in the *New Testament* book, *Acts of the Apostles*.

Thanks to Constantine's purge of Christian "heretics", however, Paul's letters survived history while the letters written by "false apostles" did not. And thanks to the bonfires of orthodox vanity, hundreds of other early Christian texts vanished forever as well. The textual scholar, Christoph Markschies, believes that 85 percent of all first and second-century Christian documents are now entirely lost to us, and this estimate applies only to those works scholars already know to have once existed.[11]

Be that as it may, there is still a large corpus of extra-canonical early Christian literature. Some formerly unknown Christian texts have been rediscovered in recent times. Other texts survived history from the beginning, but are relatively unknown. Additionally, the early orthodox heresiologists of the Church preserved fragments of lost texts by quoting from them in their own writing. They also recorded sayings attributed to Jesus which are found in no other text.

While it destroyed all heretical literature it could find, the early Church considered numerous texts sufficiently "orthodox" to merit preservation—if not worthy enough to be included in the *New Testament* canon. This whole wealth of material is generally referred to as The *New Testament Apocrypha*—or "hidden books" of the New Testament period.

In former years, scholars did not include most "heretical" literature in the official *Apocrypha*, but today almost all early Christian literature is included. Generally, *The Apocrypha* is broken down into a number of categories, the first and most important of which are gospels.

"Gospels" include those works which are specifically about Jesus or his teachings, whether they carry the name "Gospel" or not. These works include Jewish-Christian gospels, gospels under the name of an Old Testament figure, gospels in the name of Jesus, gospels attributed to the twelve apostles as a group, gospels under the name of an apostle, gospels under the name of holy women, gospels under general titles, gospels attributed to "arch-heretics", gospels under the names of their users, infancy gospels, conversations with Jesus after the resurrection—or dialogue gospels—and gospels related to the suffering of Jesus. *The Apocrypha* also contains isolated sayings of Jesus from unknown sources. These are known as "agrapha".

The *New Testament Apocrypha* includes, as well, numerous epistles (letters), apocryphons (hidden books) and apocalypses. So the total corpus of extant Christian texts is quite extensive, even though it represents only a small fraction of the total works that once existed.

Even though numerous apocryphal works have existed since antiquity, very few Christians are familiar with any of this literature because—as the designation, apocrypha, suggests—this material has been "hidden" from their eyes. While that might sound sinister in itself, the fact is that for most of its history, the Roman Catholic Church denied its faithful access to the *New Testament* itself! The invention of the printing press during the sixteenth century finally put an end to the Church's practice of keeping her flocks ignorant about the Bible and the teachings of Jesus.

Some early works were considered "secret" or "hidden" due to the title of the work itself. *The Apocryphon of James* or *The Hidden Book of James*, is just one such example. Still other works indicated that they were "secret" transmissions in the text itself. The first line of *The Gospel of Thomas*, for instance, reads: "These are the secret words that the living Jesus spoke, and Didymus Judas Thomas wrote down." The author goes on to say that "Whoever finds the interpretation of these words will not taste death."

The second line of text is key to understanding what the author means when he uses the word, "secret". *The Gospel of Thomas* was not "secret" in the sense that the author didn't want anyone outside his community to read it. It was "secret" only because most people—due to their spiritual immaturity—will not be able to correctly comprehend the true meaning of what is written. The author is challenging the reader—any reader—to look beyond the literal meaning of the words in order to discover the hidden meaning—a meaning that is apparent only to those with true spiritual understanding.

In refuting the teachings of heretics, many of the early patriarchs of orthodoxy had possession of, and quoted from, such "secret" texts for the sole purpose of arguing against them. For their part, those Christians who treasured these works answered their critics by making the point that these men—so bent on the simplistic and literal interpretation of all

7

scripture—didn't have the spiritual capacity to understand what they were reading. Such texts, then, remained secret or hidden to all but the spiritually mature.

Gnostic-Christians considered their scriptures unfathomable to all but the initiated and spiritually perceptive, but they also believed that all scripture—including the Hebrew *Bible*—held several levels of meaning. Orthodox Christians—now as well as then—have always maintained, instead, that the literal meaning of scripture is its only meaning, and have always ridiculed those who searched for deeper understanding.

The second century Church father, Irenaeus, called those who searched for additional meaning, "absolutely foolish and stupid people,"[12] and denounced the writings themselves as an "abyss of madness and blasphemy against Christ."[13] Tertullian also ridiculed anyone who sought hidden meaning in a text or in life: "Away with the man who is ever seeking, for he never finds. He seeks in places where nothing can be found."[14]

In 367 C.E., Athanasius, bishop of Alexandria, ordered the destruction of all "secret" and "hidden" texts in order to "cleanse the Church" of apocryphal books that were "filled with myths, empty and polluted."[15] This attitude of the Church's patriarchs has continued unabated until the present day. The contemporary Roman Catholic scholar, Raymond Brown, has referred to Gnostic Christian texts as "the rubbish of the second century,"[16] and the current Pope has recently declared a renewed war on heresy within American Catholic seminaries.

Elaine Pagels in *Beyond Belief, The Secret Gospel of Thomas,* remarks that "Orthodoxy tends to distrust our capacity to make such discriminations (between truth and falsity in scripture) and insists on making them for us."[17] In referring to Gnostic-Christian secret texts, she notes that "... what Christians have disparagingly called gnostic and heretical sometimes turn out to be forms of Christian teaching that are unfamiliar to us—unfamiliar precisely because of the active and successful opposition of (orthodox) Christians."[18]

Certainly Christians did not get this attitude from the historical Jesus who often taught in parables precisely so that those without spiritual understanding would not understand the point of the message, while those listeners who had "ears to hear" and "eyes to see" would comprehend the parable's hidden meaning. It is clear that Jesus taught on at least two different levels, and that he reserved his "secret" teachings for those with the ability to understand them.

In the first narrative Gospel, *Mark*, Jesus states to his closest disciples: "To you has been given the secret of the kingdom of God, but for those outside everything is in parables; so that they may indeed see but not perceive, and may indeed hear but not understand."[19] This teaching style of Jesus was not an arbitrary one, but was used to wake up his listeners. In order to understand what Jesus was teaching, the listener had to break through the confines of normal logic. Jesus used parables as theological shock therapy.

In *Parables of the Kingdom*, C. H. Dodd explains what a parable is: "At its simplest, the parable is a metaphor or simile drawn from nature or common life, arresting the hearer by its vividness or strangeness, and leaving the mind in sufficient doubt about its precise application as to tease it into active thought."[20] In juxtaposing simile and metaphor in the same parable, Jesus did not try to resolve the mental tension he created, but left it up to the listener to find the solution.

Jesus' parables incorporated exaggeration, satire, paradox, surprise and story twists. One thing his stories didn't include were resolutions. Jesus refused to supply his audiences with conclusions, but forced them instead to call upon their full intellectual/intuitive resources. With no answer provided, the listener had no choice but to use intuition, imagination and mental discipline in applying the parable to his or her life in a manner that was personally meaningful. In the end, there were no "correct" interpretations of Jesus' parables because Jesus never really explained what he meant by them.

The author of Mark's Gospel tells us on several occasions that Jesus used parables exclusively when speaking with crowds. Yet Mark claims that Jesus was willing to interpret these parables in private for the benefit of his closest disciples. Such favoritism, however, seems quite unlikely. It is very doubtful that Jesus' closest disciples were as obtuse as they are made out to be in the Gospels. If they had been, Jesus wouldn't have accepted them as disciples in the first place. And if they did not understand what he was teaching, why would they have wanted to be his disciples?

It is by no means unreasonable to suggest that Jesus taught a secret tradition to his most intimate disciples. Most Jews of Jesus' time would have had at least some familiarity with the Greek and Roman mystery religions and their secret initiations and rituals. But secret traditions were also an integral part of first century Judaism. The *Dead Sea Scrolls*, discovered at Qumran in 1947, were written a century before the birth of Jesus, and contain numerous apocryphons or "hidden books".

So the roots of Jewish mysticism—the very foundations of the Kabala—existed before the time of Jesus. And a Jewish form of Gnosticism existed alongside the Christian version during the first and second centuries.

The Hebrew root for the title "Nazarene" (a sect with which Jesus is identified in the *New Testament*) has among its other meanings, the sense of 'keeping things secret'.[21] Finally, the discovery of a fragment of a secret version of Mark's Gospel in Israel in 1945 adds further strength to the argument that Jesus taught a secret tradition.

In the single story from *Secret Mark*, Jesus is represented as a hierophant of a mystery tradition in which the initiate is required to go through six days of preparation, after which he is inducted into the mysteries of the Kingdom of God. Whether or not this fragment of text can be traced to the historical Jesus, its discovery does confirm that some early Christians believed that Jesus was associated with a secret teaching tradition.[22]

THE GOSPEL OF THE UNKNOWN JESUS

The logia—or sayings— of Jesus recorded in this present work are arranged by subject matter, and some care has been taken to make them flow in a logical manner so that they represent a consistent message. The sayings of Jesus which I have selected are but a fraction of the words attributed to Jesus in these works but they are, in my opinion, the most eloquent, profound and philosophically consistent.

The Jesus who is revealed as this text unfolds may seem to the reader radically different from the Jesus who appears in the canonical Gospels. As in orthodox Christianity, Jesus is represented as a world savior. But in the Gnostic Gospels, Jesus is savior by virtue of his bringing gnosis, or knowledge, to the world: the knowledge that God dwells within each one of us, and that the purpose of human existence is to liberate ourselves from the bonds of matter so that we can return home to the source of all Being.

The authors of virtually all ancient Gospels put words into Jesus' mouth. They based this practice on the belief that they were writing "in the spirit of Jesus". In their view, what they wrote *were* the words of Jesus, since Jesus was alive in their hearts and speaking through them.

Perhaps as few as eighteen percent of the words of Jesus in the canonical Gospels can actually be attributed to the historical person himself—at least with any degree of certainty.[23] The historicity of certain other sayings can, and are, still debated. But scholars in mainline Christian denominations generally agree that all of Jesus' references to himself as the Christ or son of God in the canonical Gospels are not his words, but those of the Christian evangelist who wrote the Gospel.

Should the reader, then, not look for the message of the historical Jesus in this modern Gospel? Yes and no. This is entirely subjective, but like the ancients, I believe that I have compiled these present sayings "in the spirit" of Jesus, and I personally believe they represent the essence of what he really taught. Moreover, these words can help illuminate many of the teachings of Jesus found in the canonical Gospels

The reader will notice that many of the sayings in this Gospel are variant forms of familiar teachings found in the canonicals. But these variants are critical. Wherever they are found in *The Gospel of Thomas*, especially, they represent the more original version of Jesus' words. In comparing the two versions, the reader can see just how much the Christian evangelists altered Jesus' message.

But the *Gospel of the Unknown Jesus* is, first and foremost, inspired spiritual literature. Ultimately, it does not matter who said or wrote a certain saying. The words either ring true, or they do not. Therein lays their "authenticity."

For me, the words in this book are sacred and eternal truths about life and humanity's place in it. In that sense, these teachings are the "word of God"—they came from a place within the human soul which is divine. These words have the power to inspire, to encourage, and very often will move us to tears. Written with great care and beauty, they represent some of the most beautiful spiritual prose ever written.

Finally, *The Gospel of the Unknown Jesus* represents the voice of long ago Christians who were silenced by other Christians who were intolerant of contrary opinions—entirely incapable of comprehending any viewpoint but their own. Because of this narrow mindedness, the words in this Gospel have been hidden from our eyes for a very long time. Now, I believe, it is time for them to take their rightful place on the pages of the *Bible of the World.*

I. THE COMING OF THE AVATAR

II. THE "I AM"

According to most modern New Testament scholars, Jesus' earliest followers—and Jesus himself—did not believe that he was the Messiah, much less God incarnate. For one to speak as an incarnation of God in first century Palestine would have been the worst kind of blasphemy, punishable by death. And Jesus was hardly unaware of that fact.

Early orthodox Christians (very few of whom were Jews) maintained that Jesus' declaration of divinity was the very reason that he was crucified. But this was hardly the case. Jesus was not stoned to death for blasphemy by Jews. He was crucified by the Romans because they perceived (wrongly) that he was a political insurrectionist.

Still, I have often wondered if it is possible that the historical Jesus did at times identify himself with God in the way any mystic would. To say "God and I are one" does not necessarily imply special divine status— just the acknowledgement that God lives in us all. Is it possible that Jesus, the mystic, was intentionally misunderstood by later Christians?

The "I am" sayings in *The Gospel of John* are certainly the most eloquent of all of Jesus' divine self-references to be found in the canonical Gospels. Gnostic-Christians used these same words in identifying Jesus as their version of Christ as well. But there is one big difference: Such statements put into Jesus' mouth by Gnostic-Christians are never meant to be read literally.

Whenever Jesus makes an "I am" declaration in the Gnostic Gospels—like Krishna in the *Bhagavad Gita*—he ceases being the human Jesus. He becomes entirely transparent to the Universe. The words are not his, but come through him. This is the moment—described in all mystical literature—when the distinction between believer and the object of belief no longer exists. Jesus is gone; there is no one home but God.

Both orthodox and Gnostic-Christians believed that Jesus was an incarnation of God. The difference is that for orthodoxy, Jesus was the one and only incarnation of God in all of human history. Gnostic-Christians, however, believed—as Hindus do—that God has incarnated many times over the ages. For the sake of the world He comes again and again—whenever and wherever He is needed.

The avatar of God takes on different bodies and different names in different times and places. Here he is known as Krishna, there as the Buddha, and somewhere else as the Christ. Yet Gnostic-Christians were not literalists. For them, the concept of the divine Christ incarnating on Earth was a metaphor, not an historical event.

III. THE SACRED WAY

I find it interesting that in the *New Testament* book, *Acts of the Apostles*, the Jesus movement in Jerusalem was known as "the Way" (Acts 9:2; 19:9; 19:23; 22:4; 24:14; 24:22). In Acts 24:14, the author further claims that "the Way" was considered a "sect" by its detractors and that its followers were persecuted—to the death—by the apostle, Paul, prior to his conversion (9:2).

At least some of Jesus' disciples after his death were known as followers of "the Way". Further evidence for this can be found in the first century training manual called the *Didache*, or *Teaching of the Twelve*

Apostles. Its opening line reads: "Two Ways there are, one of Life and one of Death, and there is a great difference between the Two Ways."[24]

In *The Gospel of Matthew,* a work favored by early Jewish Christians, Jesus also teaches that there are two ways—two paths a person can travel in life. There is the wide path, which is easy, and which is taken by many. But this path, in the end, leads to the destruction of the soul. Then there is the difficult and narrow path that leads "to life". Those who take this path are few.[25]

As we know, orthodox Christians came to see Jesus himself as the Way and, in so doing, subverted his teaching about the Way that leads to life. But his earliest followers—those who followed his teachings after he was crucified—considered "the Way" to be a program for living life successfully. To them, the narrow path—which required, at a minimum, celibacy and voluntary poverty—was the only path truly worth taking, for it led directly to the Kingdom of God.

IV. THE KINGDOM

The "Kingdom of God" was not a mythological concept invented by Christians. It was a viewpoint about the nature of reality, and it was conceived of by the historical Jesus himself. The Kingdom was Jesus' central teaching, and it is impossible to understand Jesus without first understanding what he meant by "the Kingdom".

Unfortunately, orthodox Christianity once again distorted Jesus' teaching until his concept of the Kingdom served their new Messianic and apocalyptic religion. Ask any modern Christian to define the "Kingdom of God", and he or she will probably explain that the "Kingdom" is a perfect world, ruled by God. It will come into existence only at the end of time, following on the heels of the apocalypse—the cosmic showdown between the forces of good and the forces of evil. Good will ultimately prevail, and Jesus will return to Earth to judge sinners and annihilate evildoers forever.

Yet this is not at all what Jesus meant when he spoke of the Kingdom of God. What he did mean can be summed up in a single quotation found in *The Gospel of Luke* (17:20-21). Unfortunately, most translations of *Luke* conceal the true meaning:

> The kingdom of God is not coming with signs to be
> observed; nor will they say, "Lo, here it is!" or "There!"
> for behold, the kingdom of God is in the midst of you.

As it stands, this passage makes it clear enough that Jesus did not consider the Kingdom to be some new world to come. The Kingdom was a present reality, but only those with spiritual sight could see it. God's Kingdom was everywhere, but most people could not perceive its existence.

But the full meaning of what Jesus meant by the Kingdom is not revealed in this translation of *Luke*. The Greek word meaning "in the midst of" or "among you" is "entos". But "entos" is more commonly translated as "inside" or "within", and that is how the author of Luke's Gospel is using it.[26]

Jesus was saying that if you want to find the Kingdom, the place to look for it first is within yourself. If you cannot find it there—in your heart—then you will not be able to find it anywhere else either. But if you do discover it within you, you'll also be able to see it everywhere else as well.[27] For the Kingdom is not a place, it is a state of consciousness.

The historical Jesus' central teaching was a mystical teaching, yet orthodox Christianity effectively rendered it stillborn. This saying of Jesus is ignored by most Christians—ancient and modern—who would argue that this is the only saying about the Kingdom in the Gospels which has mystical connotation, and most of the other Kingdom sayings are apocalyptic in nature.

That may be, but only because these other Kingdom sayings were either altered from the original version, or were invented by the author. This can be clearly seen by comparing the more original versions of Kingdom parables in *The Gospel of Thomas* with the same parables in the canonical Gospels.

More importantly, we can be reasonably certain that Jesus' Kingdom saying in *Luke* did, in fact, originate with the historical Jesus because the same saying appears in several other entirely independent sources. It appears in papyrus Oxyrhynchus 654, a fragment of an unknown Gospel discovered during the nineteenth century; it appears in two versions in *The Gospel of Thomas,* and it appears again in a slightly different form in *The Gospel of Mary* (Magdalene).

This Kingdom saying is also the key to unlocking the puzzle of Jesus' parables about the Kingdom. These parables—those included in this work—seem cryptic until one realizes that they are all about inner reality.

V. THE QUEST

Jesus' words, "seek and ye shall find," is one of Jesus' most famous sayings—familiar to all Christians. But not all Christians interpret these words the same way. In reading these words as a child, I never got the sense that Jesus was saying that when we seek, we will find; and when we find, we don't have to seek anymore. To me, Jesus' words suggested an endless quest for God, "truth" and the meaning of life—which is never fully knowable. But the early patriarchs of orthodoxy, being literalists, thought otherwise:

> Alienated from all truth, they deservedly wallow in
> all error, tossed to and fro by it. They think differently in
> regard to the same things at different times. And they
> never attain to a well grounded knowledge. . . . They always
> have the excuse of searching for the truth (for they are
> blind), but they never succeed in finding it.[28]

> Your object in seeking was to find. . . . Now, because
> so many other things have been taught by various
> persons, are we on that account obliged to go on seeking?
> . . . When will the seeking ever end? Where is the
> finality of belief? Where is the completion in finding?[29]

Away with the man who is ever seeking, for he never
finds. He seeks in places where nothing can be found.[30]

Those who are truly on the spiritual path know that seeking never
ends since the depth of truth is unfathomable. No matter what we think
we know, there is always more to learn. Contrary to what the Church
believes, there are no pat or simple answers to the meaning of existence.
Certainly religious dogmas do not fit the bill for many people today.

VI. IMPERMANENCE

Like Krishna, the Buddha, Lao Tzu, and spiritual mystics of all ages,
Jesus taught that the things of the world are ephemeral. They have no
ultimate reality because they are subject to change and decay. If we spend
our lives seeking after things we will always be disappointed because—
even if we find them—we will eventually lose them. The end result of
not attaining one's desires, or losing what has been attained, always
results in suffering. Like it or not, this is how the Universe works. If we
choose to ignore the way reality works, we will achieve nothing but a
wasted life. On this issue—as with many others—Jesus and the Buddha
taught essentially the same thing.

VII. IGNORANCE AND DESIRE

It is hard for us to recognize the nature of impermanence simply
because of our desire for pleasure and the need to accumulate worldly
things which we think will bring us happiness. If we lose one thing,
we buy two more things to take its place. But if we are truly honest
with ourselves, we will eventually recognize that no matter how much
we acquire, no matter how much fun we have, no matter how many
countries we visit—not one single thing brought us lasting happiness.
We do everything we can not to face the real problem: *desire itself.*

Desire is one layer of ignorance. A second layer is our belief that we
are nothing more than a body and a mind. If that is the case, then "we"

17

will certainly cease to exist some day. If, however, we come to realize that our true Self is pure spirit, and that this Self always was and always will be a part of God, then we have taken the first step toward freeing ourselves from ignorance and desire.

VIII. RENUNCIATION

Right here is where just about everybody parts company with Jesus. Jesus is just alright with me until he tells me that I have to renounce the world. Like the rich man in the Gospel story, when I hear this, I walk away sadly.

For obvious reasons, this teaching of Jesus is rarely mentioned in church circles—not by the pastor, not by the parishioners. If the subject does come up, everyone can find dozens of reasons why renunciation isn't practical in the modern world.

As with so many of his teachings, this one is disregarded by Christians who think that as long as they believe that Jesus is their Lord and savior they can dispense with his "Way". The Way of Jesus is rejected when Jesus, himself, *becomes* the Way.

Many people who are no longer Christians, but still have great respect and affection for Jesus, have just as much trouble accepting his teachings on renunciation. Of course, if we have no particular interest in becoming enlightened beings in this life-time, then we can certainly pass over this difficult teaching. But if our greatest goal in life is to become liberated from the world, then we need to carefully think about this subject.

The world's great spiritual literature claims that all of the great saints and holy people of all time were renunciates. Francis of Assisi "got it" one day, threw all his possessions out the window (literally) and walked out the door naked, never looking back. Mahatma Gandhi worked at letting go of the world more slowly, but just as systematically. When he died, Gandhi was down to just seven possessions: his spectacles, his loin cloth, his sandals, his begging bowl, and copies of the Bible, the *Bhagavad Gita,* and the *Koran.* No doubt he felt encumbered, but his life was cut short before he was able to eliminate the rest of his belongings.

But why is renunciation necessary in the first place? Mystics throughout time have maintained that no one achieves enlightenment without first having renounced the cares, relationships and enticements of the world. Ultimately, it just has to do with letting go, but Jesus tried to point out that it was also a matter of practicality. No one can serve two masters—successfully. If our time is wholly consumed with material concerns—raising a family, earning a living, making something of ourselves—we have little time to devote to our spiritual life. Certainly we cannot devote every waking moment of every day seeking to be in the divine Presence.

Buddhists point out that what we have to give up, really, are not things—but our attachment to those things. This is true, but it's very difficult not be attached to our BMW, or our new plasma TV. It can be done—it just makes the job of renunciation a whole lot more difficult.

The Buddha, himself, taught the "middle way" between strict asceticism on the one hand and materialism on the other. And so did Jesus. He taught that we could be in the world, without being of it. He occasionally shared in the fruit of the vine, and accepted a fine meal from a gracious host, but he just didn't make those things part of his life-style, and neither did the Buddha.

IX. DARKNESS AND LIGHT

The words, "light" and "darkness" are, of course, used as metaphors when speaking either about the Universe or about human nature. Lao Tzu taught that darkness is the flip side of light, and both light and darkness are *necessary* realities—at least in this universe.

Darkness and light cannot exist without one another. It's just the way the Tao, or the Universe, was put together. We didn't invent the system, but we have to live with it.

Modern psychology teaches that every human being has a shadow-self. Like it or not, there is a dark side to our nature: Me and my shadow. We cannot escape our shadow, so we have to learn how not to let it dominate us. Spiritual practice allows us to do that. With our shadow-self in check, we can allow the light within us to shine—and illuminate the world.

In Gnostic theology, the metaphor of light had a further meaning: The All was pure Light, and a "spark" of this Light was "trapped" within every human being. The object of gnosis was to release this divine spark, allowing it to return to the source of Light from which it came. Gnostics did not see the physical body as a temple of God, as much as a "prison" of flesh.

X. SOPHIA (WISDOM)

Sophia is a woman's name, but it is also a word for the divine feminine principal—in ancient Hebrew thought, in the Wisdom tradition of Jesus and in Gnostic-Christianity. Sophia is always described as feminine in ancient literature, and Sophia is often considered part of the Godhead.

It is a great loss to Western civilization that Judeo-Christianity exorcised the feminine from its theology. Both Judaism and (orthodox) Christianity did this consciously, as the feminine principal was once a part of both religions.

Besides perverting theology, eliminating the feminine principal led to the repression of women in all areas of life. Gnostic-Christians, however, were not so short sighted. They honored Sophia, just as they honored God the Mother.

We have some understanding of what it means to gain wisdom about life as we grow older. Sophia/Wisdom however, is wisdom on a much greater scale. Like the Holy Spirit, Sophia is a cosmic force. It is a quality of the divine Will. Like Vishnu in the Hindu pantheon, Sophia is the sustainer of the Universe. When we tap into the deepest part of ourselves, we also tap into Sophia. *Her* Wisdom becomes *our* wisdom.

XI. GNOSIS (KNOWLEDGE)

Gnosis, or "knowledge", has nothing to do with knowing things intellectually. Gnosis has more to do with the intuition than with the intellect. It is a knowing-ness on the deepest possible level. On one level, gnosis is spiritual perception, but it is also self-knowledge in the sense that it is the psychological awareness that the Self and God are one and the same.

In the *Bhagavad Gita*, Krishna taught Arguna that the Self (Atman) was Brahman (God). "Tat tvam asi,"—" thou art That." God, and the Self that resides within are, in reality, One and the same. To understand this experientially, not intellectually, is gnosis.

XII. LIVING IN THE KINGDOM

Spiritual understanding has to be put into practice or it's useless and meaningless. If gnosis isn't lived, then it isn't true gnosis. Every person's actions immediately betray his or her level of consciousness—every minute of every day. Negative actions do not only affect others, they affect ourselves as well. We reap what we sow. This is the law of karma, the law of cause and effect. And it is an immutable and infallible law.

Jesus' ethical teachings can be seen as roughly equivalent to the Buddhist "eightfold path":

- ◆ right belief (love God and your neighbor as yourself);
- ◆ right aspiration (seek first the Kingdom of God and all things will be added to you);
- ◆ right speech (It is not what goes into your mouth that defiles you, but what comes out);
- ◆ right conduct (what you say in words, do in deeds before everyone);
- ◆ right livelihood (if you have money, do not loan it at interest, but give it to those from whom you won't get it back);
- ◆ right endeavor (heal the sick, feed the hungry, clothe the poor);
- ◆ right mindfulness (The Kingdom of heaven is within you; and whoever knows himself will find it"); and
- ◆ right meditation ("Go into your chamber and shut the door behind you, and pray to your Father who is in secret").

None of the prescriptions about living have anything to do with being "religious". The Dali Lama doesn't go around saying, "I'm a Buddhist, so you should be a Buddhist too. The world would be much better off if everybody was a Buddhist." Instead, he says, "My religion is kindness." That's it. That's the whole teaching. Which of us wouldn't want to hang out with someone like that? Which of us wouldn't want to *be* like that?

XIII. LOVE AND COMPASSION

Love and compassion are just words. They mean nothing at all unless they become a living reality in us. But if we want love to be our reality, we will have to work very hard.

XIV. HYPOCRISY

This is the fun category, because every one of us knows plenty of hypocrites, and we are only too happy to point them out at every turn. Finding someone who isn't hypocritical—at least part of the time—would be pretty hard work.

This is just my opinion, but it seems to me that the first step on the path to the Kingdom is to accept the fact that we, ourselves, are hypocrites a good deal of the time. Walking our talk is no easy thing, and most of us are not very good at it—even though we want others to think we are.

So, if we're all in the same boat, why don't we just accept that fact, rather than trying to defend ourselves every time someone calls us on our hypocrisy? Shouldn't we be thanking the other person for holding up a mirror?

Still, the big problem with hypocrisy is that we usually don't realize we're being hypocritical at the time. It's so very easy to see hypocrisy in others and so hard to see it ourselves. Jesus' prescription for working on this is to use that moment when we are about to criticize someone, to examine ourselves instead.

XV. THE NATURE OF REALITY

The Gnostic gospels are full of information explaining Gnostic cosmology, but few of these explanations were put into the mouth of Jesus. Consequently, there are only three entries in this chapter. But they are revealing.

XVI. THE ALL

Gnostic-Christians, like Hindus, had many names for God besides "the All". Yet this term seems very useful considering that it attempts to describe an ultimate Reality that is essentially indescribable.

XVII. BECOMING ONE

Whereas Hinduism and Buddhism speak of union with the divine principle in the here and now, Gnostic literature suggests that final union with God is accomplished only when the spirit separates from the body at the time of death. And it is not clear from the literature as to whether one could achieve some sort of enlightenment prior to death.

There is also nothing in the literature to help us understand how a Gnostic achieved gnosis. No practices like yoga or meditation are described or recommended. This was probably not an oversight, however. Gnostic-Christians certainly must have had practical instructions for attaining gnosis, but just as their liturgical practices went unwritten, it is possible that instructions in yogic practices were considered far too secret and important to reveal in writing.

XIII. SUFFERING

Jesus and the Buddha are in complete agreement that suffering is caused by attachment to the material world. But it would appear that Jesus' teachings about how to deal with suffering were a little different from the Buddha's. Whereas Buddha taught that suffering could be extinguished by relinquishing attachment to the object that causes suffering, Jesus seems to be saying that one can only overcome suffering by going through it, i.e. purification through fire.

Jesus suggests that one should not resist suffering when it presents itself but should, instead, transcend suffering by understanding its true nature. In one passage in this Gospel, Jesus states that if we learn *how* to suffer, then we will no longer *be able* to suffer.

IX. DEATH

Death is everybody's biggest fear because the thought of not existing is frightening. Yet almost every religion that has ever existed has taught that fear is an inappropriate response to something that is unavoidable.

Jesus, in this Gospel, teaches that death is not possible for one who has attained true knowledge of the All. The material body dies and returns to dust because it is the nature of matter to return to its own origin. But it is also the nature of spirit to return to its own origin when the body decays and dies.

The spirit cannot die because it is a part of the Godhead which has no beginning and no end. And since spirit is the true animating principle of every human being, death holds no meaning for one who is liberated from material existence. Once we understand that our true Self is spirit, not matter, death loses its power over us.

XX. THE PASSION OF THE CHRIST

The Gnostic-Christian view of the meaning of Jesus' crucifixion has no relationship to the belief system of orthodox Christianity. To the Gnostic, Jesus did not die to save anyone from sin. The mere idea that God the Father would have required such a bloody sacrifice (of Himself?) seemed absurd and disgusting to these Christians. Perhaps because of this viewpoint, these Gnostic-Christians often proposed that Jesus both did, and did not, suffer on the cross.

Some Gnostic-Christians were considered docetists by their enemies, supposedly believing that Jesus did not have a real, human, body. From the docetic point of view, nobody suffered and nobody died on the cross.

No doubt some Gnostic-Christians did believe this, but the passages in this Gospel suggest, instead, that Jesus transcended suffering even as he was experiencing it. It was, therefore, a kind of cosmic irony that he suffered and did not suffer all at the same time. The Gnostic would have asked, "If the spirit does not die, then who was it—really—who died on the cross?"

THE HIDDEN GOD

This is the Book of the Knowledge
of the Invisible God;

it is the Book of the Knowledge
of Jesus the Living One,

by means of which all the hidden mysteries
are revealed to the elect.

Jesus is the Savior of Souls,
the Word of Life,

sent by the Father from the Light-world
to humanity,

who taught His disciples
the one and only doctrine saying,

"This is the doctrine
in which all Knowledge dwells."

(The Book of the Great Logos)

Jesus said,

*Whoever discovers
the meaning of these sayings
will not experience death*

(The Gospel of Thomas)

Preserve these mysteries
which I shall give you,
and give them to no one
lest he be worthy of them.

Give them not to father
nor to mother,
not to brother, nor to sister
nor to any family member.
Give them not
for food nor for drink,
nor for sexual favors.
Give them not for gold,
nor for silver,
nor for anything at all
of this world.

Preserve these mysteries
for the sake of the good
of the whole world.

The Two Books of Jeu

I
THE COMING OF
THE AVATAR

From the beginning of the world
he runs through the ages,
changing his form
at the same time as his name,
until in his time,
anointed of God's mercy for his toil,
he shall find his rest forever.

(The Kerymata Petrou)

So when He had seen the Grace
with which the hidden Father
had endowed Him,
He himself desired to lead back
the Universe to the hidden Father,
for the Father's will is this:
that the Universe should return
to Him.

(Untitled Apocalypse)

For their sake send me, Father!
Holding the seals I will descend.
Through the aeons will I make my way,
All the mysteries will I unlock.
The forms of the gods will I manifest.
The secrets of the sacred Way
known as Gnosis, will I transmit.

(The Naassene Psalm of the Soul)

From the place of Light
have I gone forth.
From Thee, bright habitation.
I come to feel the hearts,
to measure and try all minds,
to see in whose heart I dwell.
In whose mind I repose.
Who thinks of Me, of him I think:
Who calls my name, his name I call.
Who prays my prayer from down below,
his prayer I pray from the place of Light . . .

I came and found the truthful
and believing hearts.
Even when I was not dwelling
among them, my name was on their lips.
Thus, I took them and guided them up
to the world of Light. . .

(Mandaean liturgy)

I do not remain alone
for my Father is with Me,
we are a single One.

(*The Gospel of the Savior*)

I recognized myself,
and gathered myself
together from all sides.
I gave birth to nothing of this world,
but tore up its foundations.
I gathered together my limbs
that were scattered everywhere.
I know who you are,
for I am from the realms above.

(Agrapha)

I wandered through the worlds
and generations until I came
to the gate of Jerusalem.

(Mandaen liturgy)

As I descended no one saw me.
for I was altering my shapes,
changing from form to form.
And when I arrived at their gates
I took on the likeness of men.

(*The Second Treatise of the Great Seth*)

*Do you not know that until now
I am both here and there
with the One who sent me?*

(*The Epistula Apostolorum*)

Because of those who were sick,
I became sick.
Because of those who were hungry,
I hungered.
Because of those who were thirsty,
I was athirst.

(*Agrapha*)

For I came down to dwell
with you so that you in turn
could dwell with Me.
And, finding your houses open,
I made my home
in those of you
who were willing to receive Me
at the time of my decent.

(*The Apocryphon of James*)

42

I choose as my own,
those who are
the most worthy;
and the most worthy
are those who
my Father in heaven
has given me.

(The Gospel of the Nazareans)

Behold, I shall reveal to you
all things, my beloved.
Understand what I teach
so that you may become
as I Am.

(The (second) Apocalypse of James)

ⲧⲉⲥϩⲓⲙⲉ ... ⲛⲁⲩϣⲱⲡ[ⲉ]
ⲧⲁⲧⲟⲟⲩⲥ ⲁⲩⲉϥ ... ⲕⲁ ...
ⲁⲣⲭⲏ † ϫⲟⲙⲡⲉ ⲧⲁⲛ ...ⲉⲓ
ⲡⲉϫⲉⲓ̅ⲥ̅ ϫⲉ ⲡⲉⲛⲧⲁⲩϫⲡⲟ ... ⲕⲟⲥⲙⲟⲥ
ⲛϩⲣⲣⲙⲁⲟ ... ⲉϥⲁⲣⲛⲁ ... ⲡⲕⲟⲥⲙⲟⲥ
ⲡⲉϫⲉ ⲓ̅ⲥ̅ ϫⲉ ⲡⲓ ... ⲛⲁⲕⲟ ... ⲡⲧ̅ⲕⲁⲥ
ⲙⲡⲉⲧ ⲛ̅ⲙⲙ̅... ⲟⲥⲉⲃⲟⲗ ⲁⲩⲱ ⲡⲉⲓⲟ ... ⲉⲃⲟⲗ ⲛ̅...
ⲡⲉⲧⲛ̅ ... ϭⲛⲁⲛⲁⲩ ⲁⲛⲉⲙⲟⲩ ... ⲟⲧⲡⲉⲓ̅
ϫⲱ ⲙⲙⲟⲥ ϫⲉ ⲡⲉⲧⲟⲩ... ϥ ... ⲕⲟⲥ
ⲙⲟⲥ ⲥⲙ̅ⲡ̅ϣ̅ⲁ̅ ... ⲙⲙⲟϥ ⲁⲛϯ ⲡⲉϫⲉϥ ... ⲛⲉ
ⲛ̅ⲧⲁⲣ... ⲁⲉⲓⲟ ... ⲉⲛⲧ ... ⲡⲱⲛ ... ⲧⲁⲩⲟ
ⲛ̅ⲧ ⲯⲩⲭ ⲛ̅ⲧ ... ⲁⲉⲓ ... ⲡⲉ ... ⲁ ...
ⲛⲁⲩ ⲁⲛ ϭⲓⲛⲉϥ ... ⲁⲉⲓ ... ⲁ ... ⲉ
ⲉⲥⲛ̅ⲛⲏⲩ ⲉⲧⲁ ... ⲟⲟⲩ ⲉⲥⲛ̅ⲛⲏⲩ ⲁⲛ ...
ϭⲓⲱ ... ⲧ ⲉⲣⲟⲛ ⲉⲩⲛ̅ϭⲟⲟⲥ ⲁⲛ ϫⲉ ⲉⲓⲥ ϩ̅ⲏ̅
ⲧⲉ ⲙ̅ⲡⲓⲥⲁ ⲛⲉⲉ ⲛⲓⲙ ... ⲡⲉⲧⲛ̅ ... ⲁ ... ⲧⲁ ... ⲧⲉⲣⲟ
ⲙⲡⲉⲓⲱⲧ ... ⲉⲥⲧⲡⲟ ... ⲉⲃⲟⲗ ϩⲓϫⲙⲡⲕⲁϩ ⲁⲩⲱ
ⲣⲣⲱⲙⲉ ⲛⲁⲩ ⲉⲣⲟⲥ ⲡⲉϫⲉ ... ⲓ̅ⲱⲛ ⲡⲉ ... ⲟⲥ
ⲛⲁⲩ ϫⲉ ⲙⲁⲣⲉ ⲙⲁⲣⲓ ϩⲁⲙ ⲉⲓ ⲉⲃⲟⲗ ⲛ̅ϩⲏⲧ̅ⲛ
ϫⲉ ⲛ̅ⲥϩⲓⲟⲙⲉ ⲙ̅ⲡ̅ϣ̅ⲁ̅ ⲁⲛ ... ⲡⲱⲛ ... ⲡ ... ⲡⲉϫⲉ ⲓ̅ⲥ̅
ϫⲉ ⲉⲓⲥ ϩⲏⲏⲧⲉ ⲁⲛⲟⲕ ... ⲛⲁⲥⲱⲕ ... ⲙ̅ⲙⲟⲥ ϫⲉ
ⲉⲕⲁⲁⲥ ⲛ̅ϩⲟⲟⲩⲧ ϣⲓ ... ⲁ ...ⲉ ϯ ... ⲁⲩⲱ
ⲡⲉⲧⲱⲛ̅ϩ̅ ⲉⲛⲟⲩⲧ ⲁⲙⲉⲩ ... ⲧⲉϥ ⲉⲓ̅ⲛⲉⲙ̅
ⲙⲱⲧⲛ̅ ... ϩⲟⲟⲩ ⲧ̅ ... ⲉⲥⲓⲙⲉ ... ⲙⲡⲉⲥⲛ̅ⲙⲉ
ⲛ̅ⲥϩⲟⲟⲩⲧ ϭⲛⲁⲃⲱⲕ ... ⲟⲩⲛ̅ ... ⲙ̅ⲡⲉ ... ⲧ̅
ⲛ̅ⲁ̅ⲙⲡⲏⲩⲉ ❖❖❖ ⲁⲩ ... ⲧ̅ⲗⲓⲱ

ⲡⲉⲩⲁⲅⲅⲉⲗⲓⲟⲛ

ⲡⲕⲁⲧⲁ ⲑⲱⲙⲁⲥ

ⲟⲩⲧⲉⲃ ... ⲟⲥ ... ⲣⲓⲱⲙ ... ⲁ ... ⲧⲁⲙⲓⲉ ⲉⲣⲃⲁ ...
ⲟⲥ ⲁ ... ⲱϣ ... ⲁⲛⲟⲩ ... ⲧⲉ ... ⲧ̅ⲧⲁⲙⲓⲛⲉ
ϫⲉ ⲡⲣⲟ ... ⲗ ⲁⲩⲟ ⲉⲟⲩ ... ⲱ ... ⲥⲟ ... ϩⲙ̅
ⲧⲁⲙⲓⲉ ⲡⲣⲟⲥ ... ⲁⲩⲧ ... ⲡⲥⲟ ⲉⲙⲁ ...
ⲥⲉ ϣⲟⲟⲡ ⲛ̅ ... ⲑ̅ⲉ̅ ⲉⲧⲟⲩ ...
ⲁⲩⲱ ⲉⲧⲁⲙⲓⲉ ⲟⲛ ... ⲕ ...

I am the One who exists
In the realm of the Undivided.

(*The Gospel of Thomas*)

I am the beloved.
I am the righteous.
I am the son of the Father.
If I have come into being,
then who am I?
I am not what I appeared to be,
neither will I reveal myself
as I am.

(The (second) Apocalypse of James)

I am the Light
which shines everywhere.
I Am the All.
All things have gone forth from Me,
and all things shall return to Me.
Cleave the wood,
and I am there.
Turn the stone,
and you will find Me.

(The Gospel of Thomas)

I am in everything.
I uphold the heavens,
I am the foundation
which supports the planets,
I am the Light
that shines everywhere,
that gives joy to souls.
I am the life of the world:
I am the sap in trees,
and the sweet water
that lies beneath
the children of matter.

(Manichean psalm)

I am the One
who is with you always.
I am the Father.
I am the Mother.
I am the Son.
I am the incorruptible One
who has come to teach you
what was, and what will be,
that you may know
those things which
are hidden from you,
and to instruct you concerning the
perfection of the human race.
Therefore,
lift up your face,
that you may learn the things
that I shall teach you today,
and may tell them
to your fellow spirits . . .

(The Apocryphon of John)

I am a Lamp to you who see Me.
I am a mirror to you who know Me.
I am a door to you who knock upon Me.
I am a Way to you the wayfarer.

(*The Hymn of Jesus from the Acts of John*)

I am you, and you are Me,
and where you are, there I am.
I am sown in all things,
and when you gather Me,
it is you, yourself,
whom you gather.

(*The Gospel of Eve*)

When you see yourselves
in water or mirror,
so see Me in yourselves.

(Agrapha)

I am as near to you as
the clothing of your body.

(Coptic Psalm Book)

He who is near Me
is near the fire;
and he who is far from Me
is far from the Kingdom.

(Agrapha)

He who will drink
from my mouth
will become like Me.
I myself shall become he,
and the things that are hidden
will be revealed to him.

(*The Gospel of Thomas*)

I will give you what no eye has seen
and what no ear has heard
and what no hand has touched
and what has never occurred
to the human mind.

(The Gospel of Thomas)

Come to Me, for my yoke is easy
and my lordship is gentle,
and you will find rest
for yourselves.

(The Gospel of Thomas)

You have Me for a couch;
rest yourselves upon Me.

(The Hymn of Jesus from the Acts of John)

Rest yourselves by the spring
of the water of Life.

(The Gospel of the Savior)

Now if you follow My dance,
see yourselves in Me
who am speaking.

(The Hymn of Jesus from The Acts of John)

See yourself in Me who speaks;
and seeing what I do,
keep silence
on my mysteries.

(The Hymn of Jesus from The Acts of John)

III

THE SACRED WAY

I am a door to those who knock on Me.
I am a Way to you the traveler.

(The Hymn of Jesus from the Acts of John)

*When I came, I revealed the Way
and taught them about the path
that must be traveled—
the chosen and solitary ones
who have known the Father,
because they have believed
in the truth.*

(*Dialogue of the Savior*)

Judas said,
"Tell me Lord, what is the beginning
of the Way?"

Jesus answered,
"Love and goodness.
For if one of these had existed
among those who rule,
evil would never
have come into existence."

(Dialogue of the Savior)

Seek your salvation without being urged.
Rather, desire it of your own accord
and, if possible, attain this goal
even before Me: for because of this
the Father will love you.

(The Apocryphon of James)

Without waiting or hesitating,
and without consideration of those around you,
follow the Way that is direct
and straight and narrow.

(*The Epistula Apostolorum*)

Be prepared in the face of all things.
Happy is the man who came upon the war
and observed the battle with his own eyes.
He did not kill. Neither was he killed,
yet he came forth victoriously.

(Dialogue of the Savior)

Cling to the holy ones,
for they who do so
are themselves made holy.

(Agrapha)

Abandon the difficult way
which has so many forms,
and walk with Him
who wants you to become
free men with Me.

(Dialogue of the Savior)

You have known the Way,
the one angels and authorities
have not known.
It is from the Father and the Son
because they are One.
And you will travel on this
Way you have known.

(Dialogue of the Savior)

IV
THE KINGDOM

The Kingdom is within you,
and whoever knows oneself
will find it.
All those who find the Kingdom
will know that they are
heirs of the Father,
Know that you are in God,
and God is in you.

(Papyrus Oxyrhynchus)

The Kingdom will not come
when you expect it.
No one will say, "Look it is here!"
or "See, it is over there."
Instead, the Kingdom of the Father
is spread out over the whole world,
and people do not see it.

(The Gospel of Thomas)

If those who seek to attract you say
"Look, the Kingdom is in the heavens"
then the birds of heaven
will be there before you.
If they say "It is under the earth"
then the fish of the sea
will get there before you do.
In fact, the Kingdom
is within you,
and all around you.

(The Gospel of (Thomas)

*Take care that no one
deceives you by saying,
"Look over here!" "Look over there!"
For the true child
of humanity is within you.
Follow it.
For those who seek it
will find it.*

(The Gospel of Mary (Magdalene))

Arise, and I will reveal to you
what is beyond heaven,
and what is within heaven,
and your rest that is in
the Kingdom of heaven.

(The Epistula Apostolorum)

His disciples said,
"What is the Kingdom like?"
Jesus answered,
"The Kingdom is like a shepherd
who had a hundred sheep.
The largest among the sheep went astray.
The shepherd left the ninety-nine sheep
and searched for the one until he found it.
After he had gone to all this
trouble he said to the sheep,
I love you more than the
the ninety-nine.

(The Gospel of Thomas)

The Kingdom is like a woman
who hid leaven in dough,
making it into large loaves.
Anyone with ears, should hear.

(The Gospel of Thomas)

The Kingdom is like a merchant
who discovered a pearl
among his consigned goods.
The merchant was wise.
He sold the goods,
but bought the pearl for himself.
You, too, should seek the enduring treasure
which does not perish, and which
no moth eats, and no worm destroys.

(The Gospel of Thomas)

The Kingdom is like a man
who had a treasure hidden in his field
without knowing of it.
The man died and left the field
to his son, who also
did not know about the treasure.
The son sold the field,
and the one who bought it
found the treasure while he was plowing.
He began to loan money with interest
to whomever he wished.

(The Gospel of Thomas)

The Kingdom of the Father
can be compared
to a man who had good seed.
His enemy came by night
and sowed weeds among the good seed.
The man did not permit his workers
to pull up the weeds, but said to them,
"I am afraid that if you pull up the weeds
you will pull up the grain as well.
But on the day of the harvest
the weeds will be in plain sight,
then they can be pulled up and burned."

(The Gospel of Thomas)

The Kingdom of the Father is like a woman
who was carrying a vessel full of grain.
While she was walking on the road,
the handle of the vessel broke;
the grain spilled out behind her on the road.
Not being aware of the accident,
she did not notice it.
When she arrived home
she put the jar down
only to find that it was empty.

(The Gospel of Thomas)

The Kingdom is like a mustard seed.
It is the smallest of all seeds.
But when it falls on soil
that has been tilled,
it grows into a large plant
and becomes a shelter for the
birds of heaven.

(*The Gospel of Thomas*)

The Kingdom is like a fisherman
who cast his net into the sea.
When he drew the net up,
it was full of small fish.
Among them was one large fish.
He threw all the small fish
back into the sea,
and chose the large fish
without hesitating.
Those who have ears,
let them hear.

(The Gospel of Thomas)

When the Lord was asked by a man
when his Kingdom would come,
He answered him:
When the two shall become one,
and when what is on the outside
becomes like what is on the inside,
and when male and the female
are no longer male and female.

(Agrapha)

Jesus saw small children being nursed
and said to his disciples,
"These infants being nursed are like those
who enter the Kingdom of God."
His disciples asked him,
"Must we become children
in order to enter the Kingdom?"
Jesus answered them and said,
"What you must do is to unify
that which is outside you
with that which is within; that which is above you
with that which is below.
You must make the male and female
one and the same.
Then you will be able to enter the Kingdom.

(The Gospel of Thomas)

Do not let the Kingdom of heaven
die within you.
For the Kingdom is like the shoot
of a palm tree,
where its fruit had fallen
down around it.
The fruit gave forth seeds,
and after they sprouted,
they caused their womb
to become barren.

(The Apocryphon of James)

V

THE QUEST

Seek and you will find.
But what you asked Me about
in earlier times, and which
I did not tell you until now,
I now want to tell you
so that you will not have to
seek them any longer.

(The Gospel of Thomas)

Whoever seeks will find.
It will be opened to him.

(The Gospel of Thomas)

Let him who seeks
never cease until he finds,
and when he finds
he will wonder,
and wondering he will reign,
and reigning, he will rest.

(Oxyrhynchus logia)

Seek after the great things,
and the lesser things
will be given you;
seek for those things of heaven,
and the earthly will be given you.

(Agrapha)

*All who seek the truth
from a place of wisdom
will make themselves wings
so as to flee the passions
which consume the essential
nature of all living beings.*

(The Book of Thomas the Contender)

But if the things that are visible to you
are unseen by you,
how can you understand
the things that are not visible?

(The Book of Thomas the Contender)

Understand what is
in front of your face,
and that which is hidden
from you
will be revealed.

(Kephalaia)

*Everything that is not
visible to you, but is hidden,
will become plain to you.
For there is nothing hidden
which will not be made manifest,
there is nothing buried
which will not be raised.*

(Oxyrhynchus logia)

The disciples asked,
"When will you be revealed to us
and when will we see you?"

Jesus said,
""When you go forth
naked and unashamed.
When you take your outer garments
and walk on them like children do.
Then you will become children
of the living God."

(The Gospel of Thomas)

*Preserve those things
that can follow you,
and seek them out,
and speak from within those things,
so that there is harmony within you!
For I tell you the truth,
the living God is in you,
and you are in Him.*

(Dialogue of the Savior)

Mary said,
"Lord, is there a place
which is lacking truth?"
The Lord said,
"The place where I am not."

(Dialogue of the Savior)

That which you seek
and ask about,
behold,
it is within you.

(Dialogue of the Savior)

VI

IMPERMANENCE

It has bound them with its chains;
and held their limbs immobile
through desire for those
visible things which perish,
change and are transformed.

(The Gospel of the Egyptians)

Now, that which changes
will decay and perish.

(The Book of Thomas the Contender)

Visible things that decay and change
and go their way through impulse
have always been attracted downwards.
When they are destroyed,
they become one
with all the beasts of the
perishable realm.

(The Book of Thomas the Contender)

Therefore, I say to you,
be sober; do not be deceived!

(The Apocryphon of James)

There was a rich man
who had much money.
He said,
"I shall put my money to use
so that I may sow,
reap, plant, and fill
my storehouse with produce.
Then I will be secure.
Those were his intentions,
but that very night he died.
Let him who has ears, hear.

(The Gospel of Thomas)

Because these visible bodies
eat those creatures like themselves,
their bodies change.
And that which changes
will perish and disappear.

(The Book of Thomas the Contender)

This is why you get sick and die:
because you love the things
which deceive you.
Anyone who has the ability to think
should consider this.

(The Gospel of Mary)

*Therefore,
while you are in the body,
do not let matter rule over you.*

(The Gospel of the Savior)

*Everything that comes
from the perishable will perish.
But what comes from Spirit
does not perish
but becomes imperishable.
Many have gone astray because
they did not know this difference,
and they died.*

(The Sophia of Jesus Christ)

The visible parts of a person
will dissolve.
This vessel of flesh will perish.
And even when it disintegrates
it remains part of the visible world,
of things which can be seen.

And then the visible fire gives them pain.
And because of their desire for visible things,
they are brought back into the visible world.

(The Book of Thomas the Contender)

Have confidence
and be of a peaceful heart.
Truly I say to you,
your rest will be in heaven
in the place where there is
neither eating nor drinking,
neither rejoicing nor mourning,
nor perishing of those who are in it.

(The Epistula Apostolorum)

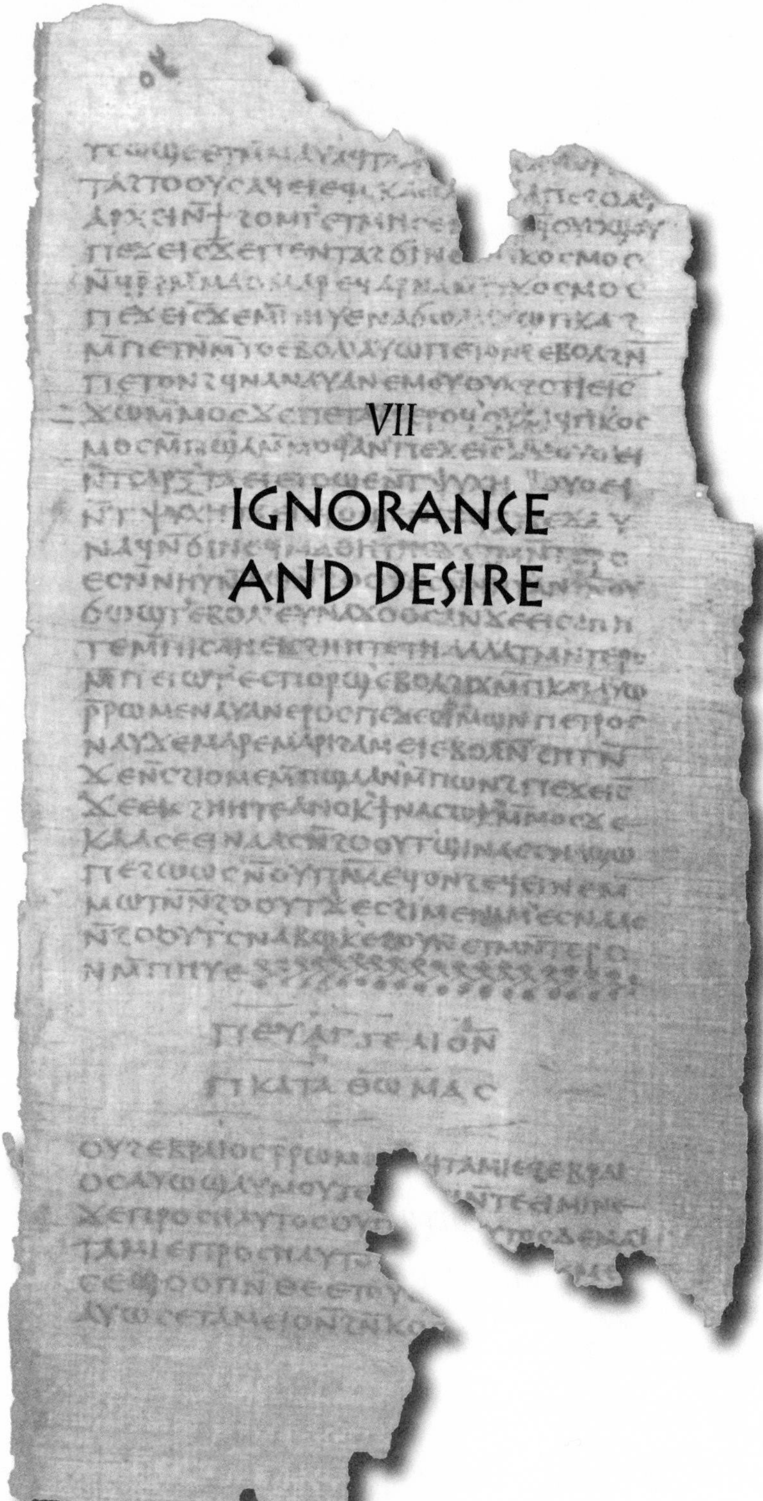

VII

IGNORANCE
AND DESIRE

*How sad it is for you who hope in the flesh
and are attached to the prison that will perish.
How long will you remain in ignorance?
Your hope is for the things of this world,
and your god is this life.
You are corrupting your souls!*

(The Book of Thomas the Contender)

How sad it is for you within whom
the insatiable fire burns.

How sad for you because
of the wheel that turns
in your minds!

This fire will devour
your flesh openly
and your souls secretly,
and doom you to the fate
of those like you.

(The Book of Thomas the Contender)

My heart grieves
for the souls of humanity,
because they are blind
in their hearts and do not see.

(Agrapha)

If you do not fast from the world
you will not find the Kingdom of God,
and if you do not keep the Sabbath
all week long,
you will not see the Father.

(Oxyrhynchus logia)

The mother and brothers of Jesus said to him:
"John the Baptist baptizes for the remission of sins.
Let us go and be baptized by him."
But Jesus said to them,
"How have I sinned that I need
to be baptized by him?
Unless what I have said is ignorance."

(Agrapha)

VIII

RENUNCIATION

While you are in the body,
do not let matter rule over you.

(The Gospel of the Savior)

Among these transitory things
which are not yours,
seek for the things of your own—
those things that will not pass away.

(Agrapha)

For those who seek Life,
this is their wealth.
For the pleasures
of the world are false;
and its gold and silver
are a delusion.

(Dialogue of the Savior)

Possess nothing on earth.

(Agrapha)

Have no care from morning to evening,
and from evening to morning,
about what you shall put on.

(The Gospel of Thomas)

For what is the profit
if one gains the whole world
and loses his own soul?

(The Gospel of the Egyptians)

Do not be afraid;
I am rich.
I will fill you
with my wealth.

(*The Gospel of the Savior*)

*Blessed are the poor ones,
for yours is the Kingdom of heaven*

(The Gospel of Thomas)

*Blessed is the one who
crucifies the world,
and does not let the world
crucify him.*

(The Book of the Great Logos)

*I have overcome the world.
Do not let the world overcome you.
I have become free of the world.
You too become free of it.*

(The Gospel of the Savior)

Matthew said,
"How does the small join itself to the Great?"
He said,
"Abandon the works
which that cannot follow you.
Then you will rest."

(Dialogue of the Savior)

A rich man said to Jesus:
"Master, what must I do to gain Life?"
Jesus said to him:
"Uphold the law and the prophets."
The rich man answered: I have done this."
Jesus said,
"Then go and sell all of your possessions,
and afterward, come and follow me."
But the rich man was silent because
this saying did not please him.
And Jesus said,
"How can you say that you have
fulfilled the Law and prophets
when it stands written in the Law,
'Love your neighbor as yourself'?'
Look around you. Many of your
brothers who are all sons of Abraham
are living in squalor and dying of hunger.
Your house is full of many good things,
yet you give none of them to those in need."
Jesus turned and said to Simon, his disciple,
"It is easier for a camel to go through
the eye of a needle than for a rich man
to enter the Kingdom of heaven."

(Agrapha)

Anyone who will leave father and mother,
brother and sister, wife and child,
and possessions,
and willingly takes up his cross
and follows Me,
will receive all that I have promised.
And I will reveal to such a one
the mystery of the hidden Father.

(An Untitled Apocalypse)

If the owner of a house knows
that a thief is coming,
he will stand guard and not let him
into his house to steal his goods.

Guard yourselves, then, against the world.
Arm yourself, and be prepared, so that thieves cannot
find a way to invade your domain,
Otherwise the problems you fear
will surely come about.

(The Gospel of Thomas)

Let him who is rich become king,
and let him who has power,
renounce it.

(The Gospel of Thomas)

The disciples of John marry
and are given in marriage,
but my disciples are as the
angels of God in heaven.

(The Book of John the Evangelist)

He that is married
should not renounce his wife,
and he who has not married
should not marry.

(The Gospel of the Egyptians)

Keep your flesh pure.

(Agrapha)

Become passers-by.

(The Gospel of Thomas)

The world is a bridge.
Cross over it,
do not install yourself upon it.

(Agrapha)

IX

DARKNESS AND LIGHT

It is in *Light* that *Light* exists.

(The Book of Thomas the Contender)

The images of the material world
are manifest to anyone,
but the *Light* in them remains
hidden within the Image
of the Father.
He is manifest,
but his Image remains
hidden by his *Light*.

(The Gospel of Thomas)

Fear not the destruction of the body,
but fear the power of darkness.

(Coptic logia)

If one does not stand
in the darkness,
he will not be able
to see the Light.

(Dialogue of the Savior)

For you, the darkness
was the same as the light
because you exchanged
your freedom for slavery!
You gave your hearts
over to darkness
and surrendered your thoughts
to folly.

(The Book of Thomas the Contender)

His disciples said to him,
"Show us where You are,
for we wish to find that place."

He said to them,
"Whoever has ears, let him hear.
Light exists within an enlightened man,
and it lights up the whole world.
But if that Light does not shine,
then there is nothing
in that man but darkness."

(The Gospel of Thomas)

When a blind man and one who sees
stand together in the darkness,
there is no difference between them.
But when the Light comes,
the man who sees
will recognize the Light,
while the blind man
will remain in darkness.

(The Gospel of Philip)

If a man is in harmony
within himself,
he will be filled with light,
but if he has not achieved
this inner harmony
he will be filled with darkness.

(The Gospel of Thomas)

I am a Lamp
to those who see Me.

(*The Hymn of Jesus from the Acts of John*)

The lamp of the body is the mind.
As long as you have harmony within yourself,
your bodies will be full of light.
But if your hearts are dark,
the enlightenment you hope for
will not manifest itself.

(*Dialogue of the Savior*)

*Preach from the housetops
that which you have come to understand.
No one lights a lamp and hides it.
Neither do they put it in a hidden place.
Instead, they fix it to a lampstand
so that everyone who enters and leaves
will see it.*

(*The Gospel of Thomas*)

This visible light shines for you
—not so that you will remain here,
but so that you might transcend
the darkness.

When all spirits transcend
the powers of the material realm,
the Light will withdraw itself
up to its Essence,
and its Essence will welcome it,
for it is a good servant.

(The Book of Thomas the Contender)

Do not grieve the Holy Spirit
which is within you,
and do not extinguish
the Light that shines forth in you.

(*Agrapha*)

Let all of you seek the Light,
so that the power of the stars—
which exists within you—may live.

(*The Pistis Sophia*)

If they say to you,
"Where did you come from?"
say to them,
"We came from the Light,
the place where Light
came into being
of its own accord."

(The Gospel of Thomas)

X
SOPHIA (WISDOM)

ⲡⲉⲩⲁⲅⲅⲉⲗⲓⲟⲛ

ⲡⲕⲁⲧⲁ ⲑⲱⲙⲁⲥ

Wisdom sends forth her children.

(*Agrapha*)

*Truth seeks out
the wise and the righteous.*

(*Dialogue of the Savior*)

Blessed are those who are wise
and seek the truth.
For when they find it
they will rest in it forever,
and will not be afraid of those
who cause disturbance.

(The Book of Thomas the Contender)

Be as wise as serpents
and as innocent as doves.

(The Gospel of Thomas)

It is impossible for a wise person
to live with a fool.
For the wise person is guided by wisdom,
while to the fool, good and the bad
are the same.

The wise person is nourished
by the truth,
and becomes like a tree that
grows by a turbulent stream.

(The Book of Thomas the Contender)

Seeing a man
working on the Sabbath,
he said to him:
"Man, if you understand what
you are doing then you are blessed;
but if you do not know,
then you are as one cursed
and a transgressor of the law."

(Agrapha)

If a blind man leads a blind man,
they will both stumble and fall.

(The Gospel of Thomas)

*An old man
will not hesitate to ask
a small child seven days old
about the place in life,
and he will live.
For many who are first
will become last,
and those two will become
one and the same.*

(The Gospel of Thomas)

If you who seek to be greater,
become less,
then when you are invited
to dine at someone's table,
you will not seat yourself
in a prominent place—
since someone more important
than you might come in,
and the host might say to you,
"Move down."
Then you will be put to shame.
So seat yourself
in a less prominent place,
so that if someone of lesser stature
than you comes in,
the host will say to you,
"Move up to a higher place";
and this will be profitable to you.

(Codex Bezae)

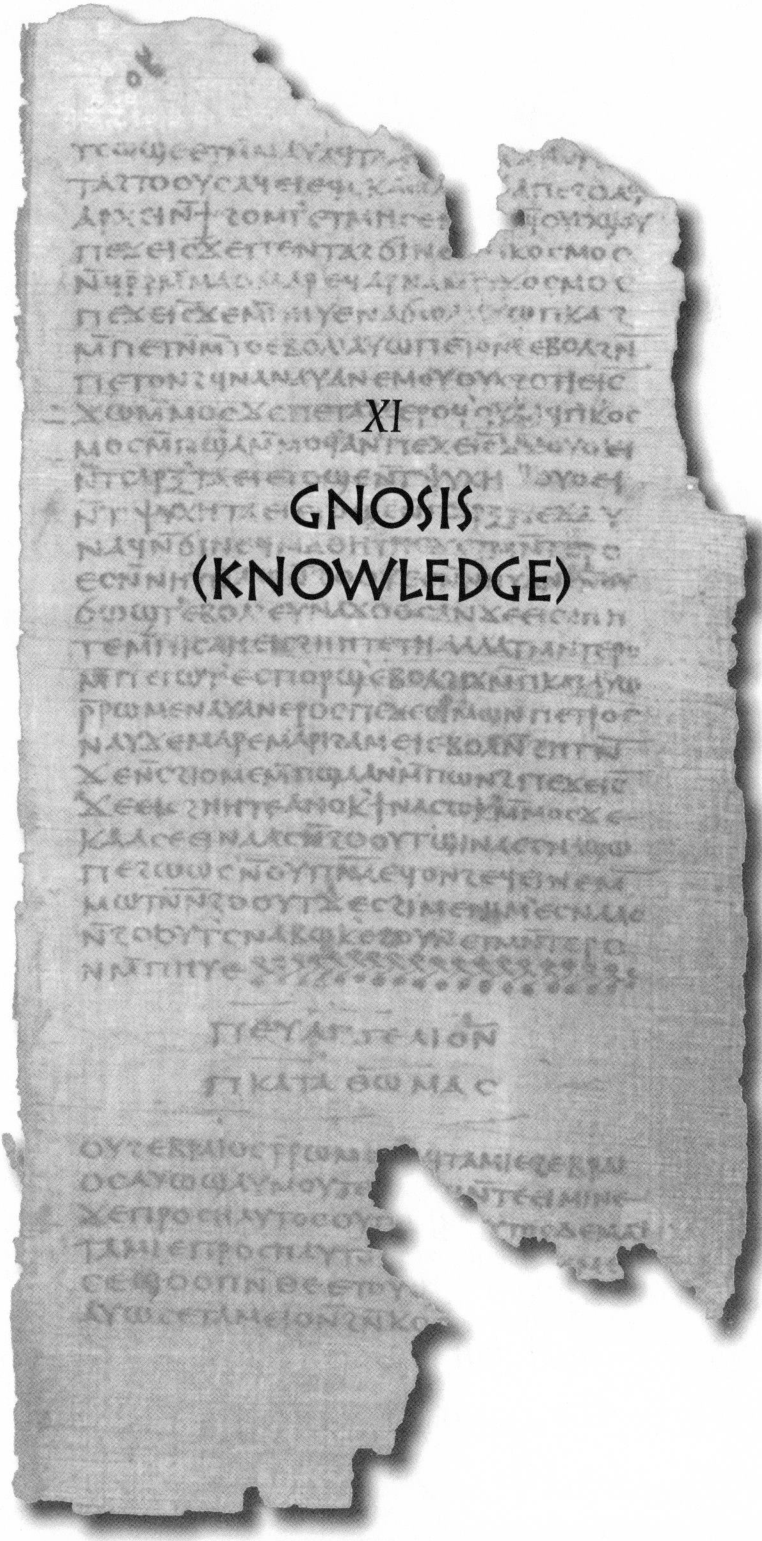

XI

GNOSIS (KNOWLEDGE)

*Go into your chamber
and shut the door behind you,
and pray to your Father
who is in secret.*

(The Gospel of Philip)

*The Kingdom of Heaven
is within you;
and whoever knows himself
will find it.
Strive, therefore, to know yourselves,
and you will become aware
that you are children of the living Father;
and you will know that you are
living in the City of God,
and that you are that City.*

(An Oxyrhynchus Papyrus)

When you know yourselves,
you will be known,
and you will know that
you are children of the
living Father.
But if you do not know
yourselves, you live in poverty
and you yourselves are poverty.

(The Gospel of Thomas)

*Anyone who has not known themselves
has known nothing.
But those who have known themselves
have already achieved knowledge
of the All.*

(*The Book of Thomas the Contender*)

If one does not understand
the nature of fire,
he will burn in it . . .
If one does not understand
the nature of water,
he drown in it . . .
If one does not understand
the nature of blowing wind
he will blow away with it.
If one does not understand
how the body, which he bears,
came into existence,
he will die along with it.
And if someone
does not know the Son
how will he know the Father?
And to those who do not understand
the nature of all things,
they remain hidden.
If one does not understand
how he came into existence,
he will not understand
how he ceases to exist.

(Dialogue of the Savior)

You study the heavens
and the earth,
but you do not know
what is in front of your face,
nor do you understand
the present time.

(*The Gospel of Thomas*)

Whoever has come to understand
the world has discovered
something without Life.
And anyone who has discovered this
is superior to the world.

(The Gospel of Thomas)

You have understood
the things I have said to you
and accepted them
on faith.
If you have truly known them,
then they are yours to keep.
If not, then they are not yours at all.

(*Dialogue of the Savior*)

Understand what is in
front of you
and that which is hidden
from you will become apparent.
For there is nothing
hidden that will not
be revealed.

(The Gospel of Thomas)

*One who sees himself
only on the outside,
not within,
becomes small himself
and makes others small.*

(The Gospel of Man)

If you do not transform the things
that are below into the things
which are above,
and the things above into
the things below,
and transform the right into the left,
and the left into the right,
and what is before into what is behind,
and what is behind into what is before,
you cannot enter
the Kingdom of God.

(*Agrapha*)

When you reveal
what is within you,
what you have manifested
will save you.
But what you have within you
will kill you
if you do not know that
it is within you.

(The Gospel of Thomas)

The little children teach
the grey-haired old men.
Those who are six years old
teach those who are sixty.

(Coptic Psalm Book)

His disciples said to him,
"Twenty-four prophets spoke in Israel
and they all spoke of you."
He said to them,
"You have left out the
One living in your presence
and have spoken only of the dead."

(The Gospel of Thomas)

Seek to see Him who is Living,
while you are living, lest you die
and seek Him when you can
no longer find Him.

(The Gospel of Thomas)

The Pharisees and the scribes
have taken the keys of Knowledge
and hidden them.
They have not entered,
nor have they permitted entry
to those who wished to enter.
But you, be as prudent as serpents
and as simple as doves.

(The Gospel of Thomas)

They said to him,
"Tell us who You are
so that we may believe in You."
He said to them,
"You examine the appearance
of heaven and earth,
but He who is in front of you,
you do not recognize,
and you do not know how
to interpret this moment."

(The Gospel of Thomas)

Listen to the word!
Understand Gnosis!
Love life—
and no one will persecute
or oppress you,
other than you yourselves.

(The Apocryphon of James)

XII

LIVING IN THE KINGDOM

His disciples asked him,
"Do you want us to fast?
How should we pray?
Should we give to charity?
What diet shall we observe?"
Jesus said,
"Do not tell lies,
and do not do what
you hate,
for all things are visible
in the sight of Heaven."

(The Gospel of Thomas)

If your brother has sinned
by what he has said,
and has apologized,
accept him seven times in a day.
The disciples said to him,
"Seven times in a day?"
The Lord answered,
"Yes, even seventy times seven,
for even the prophets who were
anointed by the Holy Spirit
were not yet perfect."

(*The Gospel of the Nazareans*)

Wherever you go
where others receive you,
eat what they set before you,
and heal the sick among them.
What goes into your mouth
will not make you unclean.
Rather it is what comes
out of your mouth
that makes you unclean.

(The Gospel of Thomas)

If you have money,
do not loan it at interest,
but give it to someone from
whom you will not get it back.

(The Gospel of Thomas)

What you say with words,
do in deeds before everyone.

(Agrapha)

No one can mount two horses
or stretch two bows.
Neither is it possible for a servant
to serve two masters;
he will honor the one
and treat the other badly.

No one drinks old wine
and then immediately wants
to drink new wine.
Neither is new wine put
into old wineskins,
because they might burst;
nor is old wine put
into a new wineskins,
because it might spoil.

An old patch is not
sewn onto a new garment,
because a tear would result.

(The Gospel of Thomas)

Do not return evil for evil,
or insult for insult,
or fist for fist,
or curse for curse.

(*Agrapha*)

Blessed are they who mourn
over the destruction of unbelievers.

(*Agrapha*)

You are the key who
opens the door for every man,
and shuts it for every man.

(*Agrapha*)

Become better than I!
Make yourselves like
the children
of the Holy Spirit.

(*The Apocryphon of James*)

XIII

LOVE AND COMPASSION

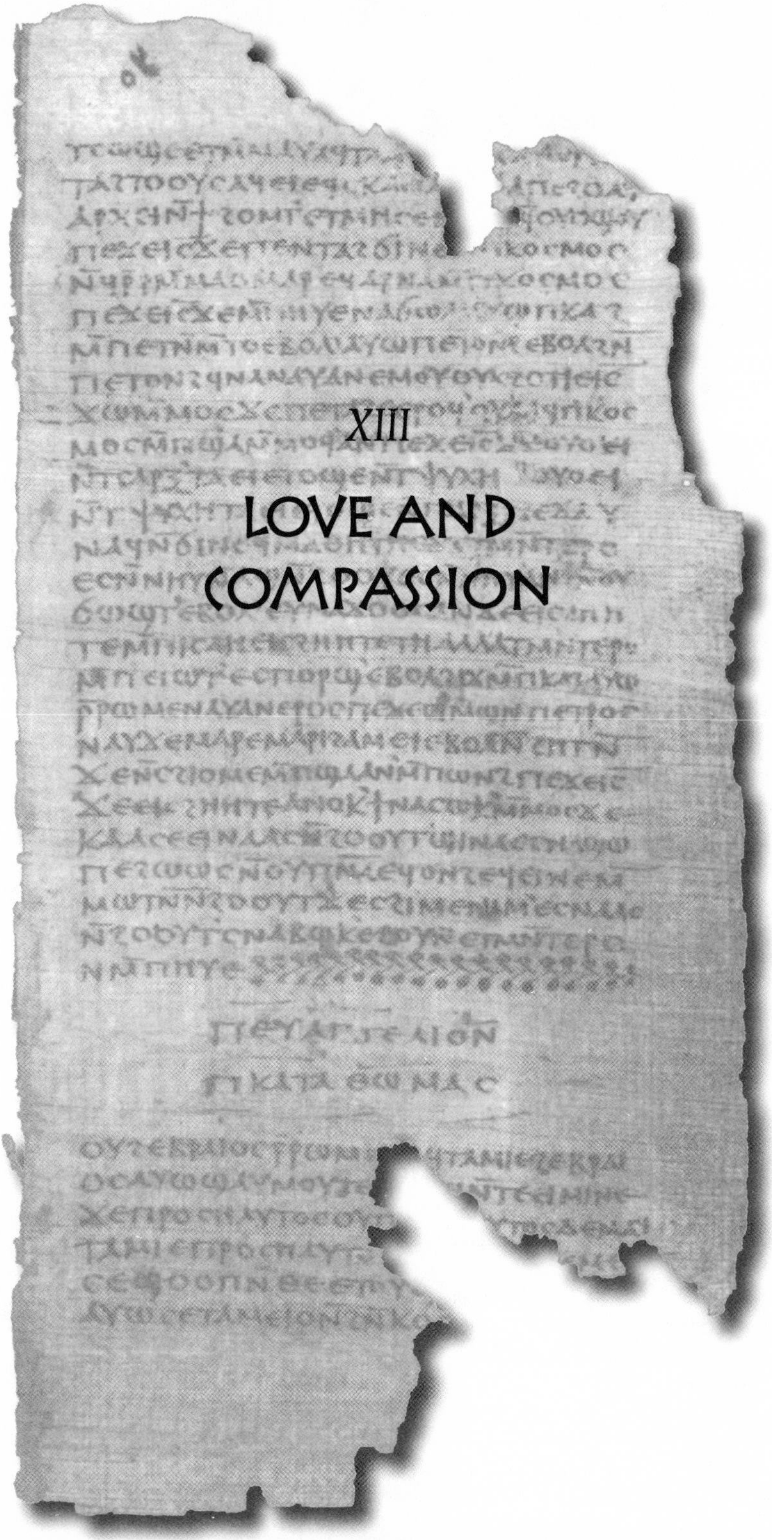

Be earnest about the Word!
For as to the Word, its first part
is faith; the second, love;
the third, works;
for from these come life.

(The Apocryphon of James)

Where love is little,
all acts are imperfect.

(The Gospel of Mani)

How does it benefit you
if you love only those
who love you?
Rather, it will benefit you
if you love your enemies
and those who hate you.

(The Gospel of the Egyptians)

Love your brother
like your soul,
guard him like
the pupil of your eye.

(The Gospel of Thomas)

Be glad only when you look upon your brother with love.

(The Gospel of the Hebrews)

Love hides a multitude of sins.

(Agrapha)

Be merciful that you may obtain mercy;
forgive so that you may be forgiven;
whatever you do, will be done to you;
as you judge, you will be judged;
as you do service,
so will service be done to you;
whatever you measure out,
will be measured out
to you in return.

(Agrapha)

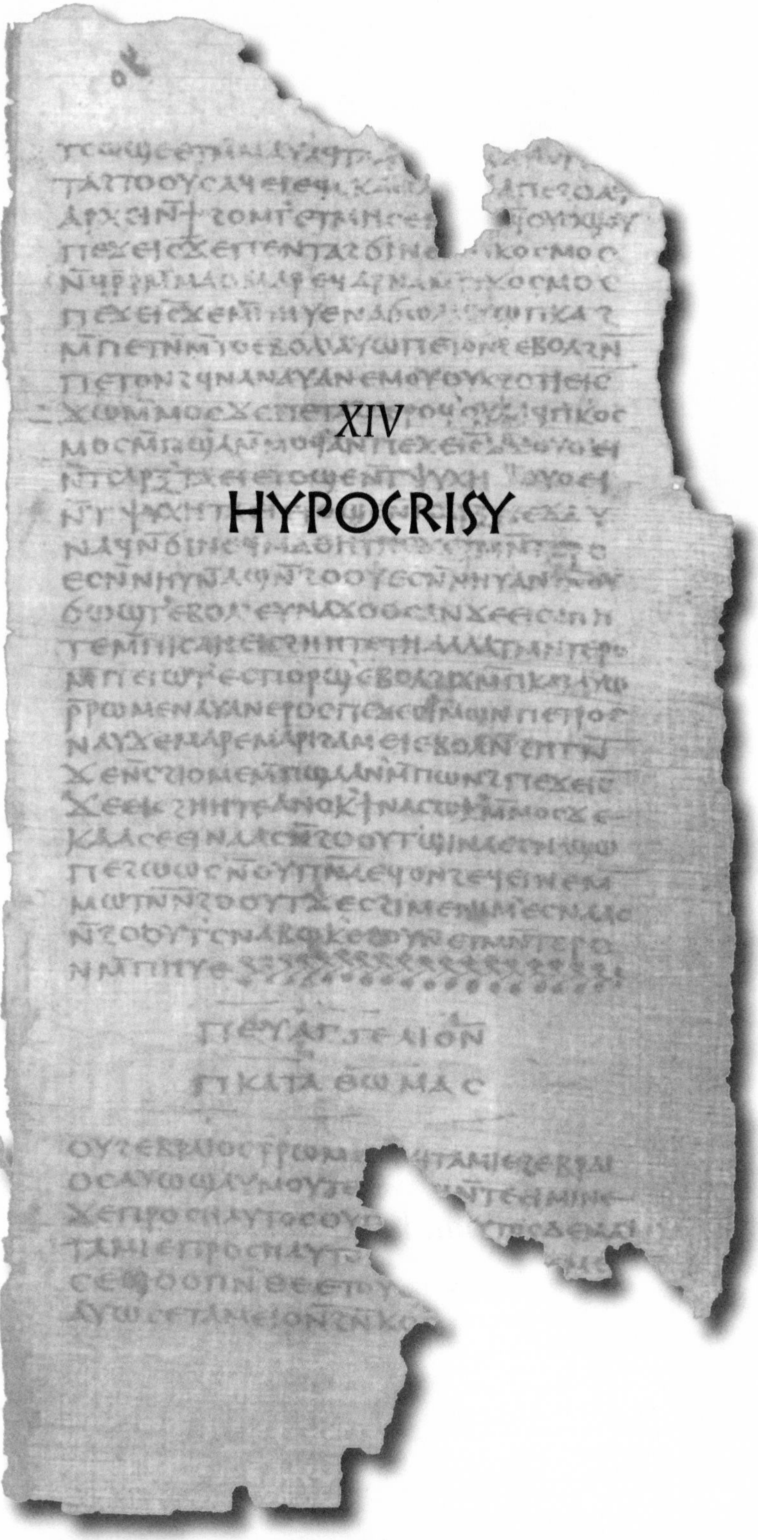

XIV
HYPOCRISY

Reject hypocrisy and evil thought,
for it is thinking that gives birth
to hypocrisy; and hypocrisy is far
from the truth.

(*The Apocryphon of James*)

Why do you wash the
outside of the cup,
and do not recognize that He
who made the inside
also made the outside?

(*The Gospel of Thomas*)

You are able to see the speck
in your brother's eye,
but you entirely miss the beam
in your own eye.
When you remove the beam
from your own eye,
then you will see clearly enough
to remove the speck
from your brother's eye.

(The Gospel of Thomas)

His disciples said to him,
"Who are You, that You
say these things to us?"
Jesus said to them,
"You do not recognize who I am
by what I say to you.
You have become like the Jews,
who love the tree and hate the fruit
or love the fruit and hate the tree."

(The Gospel of Thomas)

His disciples said to him,
"Is circumcision beneficial or not?"
He said to them,
"If it were beneficial,
the Father would create men
already circumcised.
True circumcision
is circumcision of the spirit."

(The Gospel of Thomas)

The Pharisees are like dogs
sleeping in the manger of oxen,
They do not eat,
neither do they let the oxen eat.

(The Gospel of Thomas)

I have come to end sacrifices,
and if you do not cease from sacrificing,
the wrath of God will not cease from you.

(The Gospel of the Ebionites)

XV

THE NATURE OF REALITY

All elements, all structures,
and all creatures
exist in and with one another,
and they will return again
to their own Source.
For the nature of matter returns to
the source of its own nature.
He who has ears to hear, let him hear.

(The Gospel of Mary)

There is no such thing as "sin".
It is you who create "sin"
when you do things that mix
the natural with the unnatural,
like adultery,
which is called "sin".

(The Gospel of Mary)

The apostles asked Jesus about
the life of inanimate nature,
whereupon he said:
"If that which is inanimate
is separated from the living
element which is commingled with it,
and appears alone by itself,
it is again inanimate and
not capable of living,
while the living element which
has left it, retaining its
vital energy unimpaired,
never dies."

(The Book of Mysteries)

XVI

THE ALL

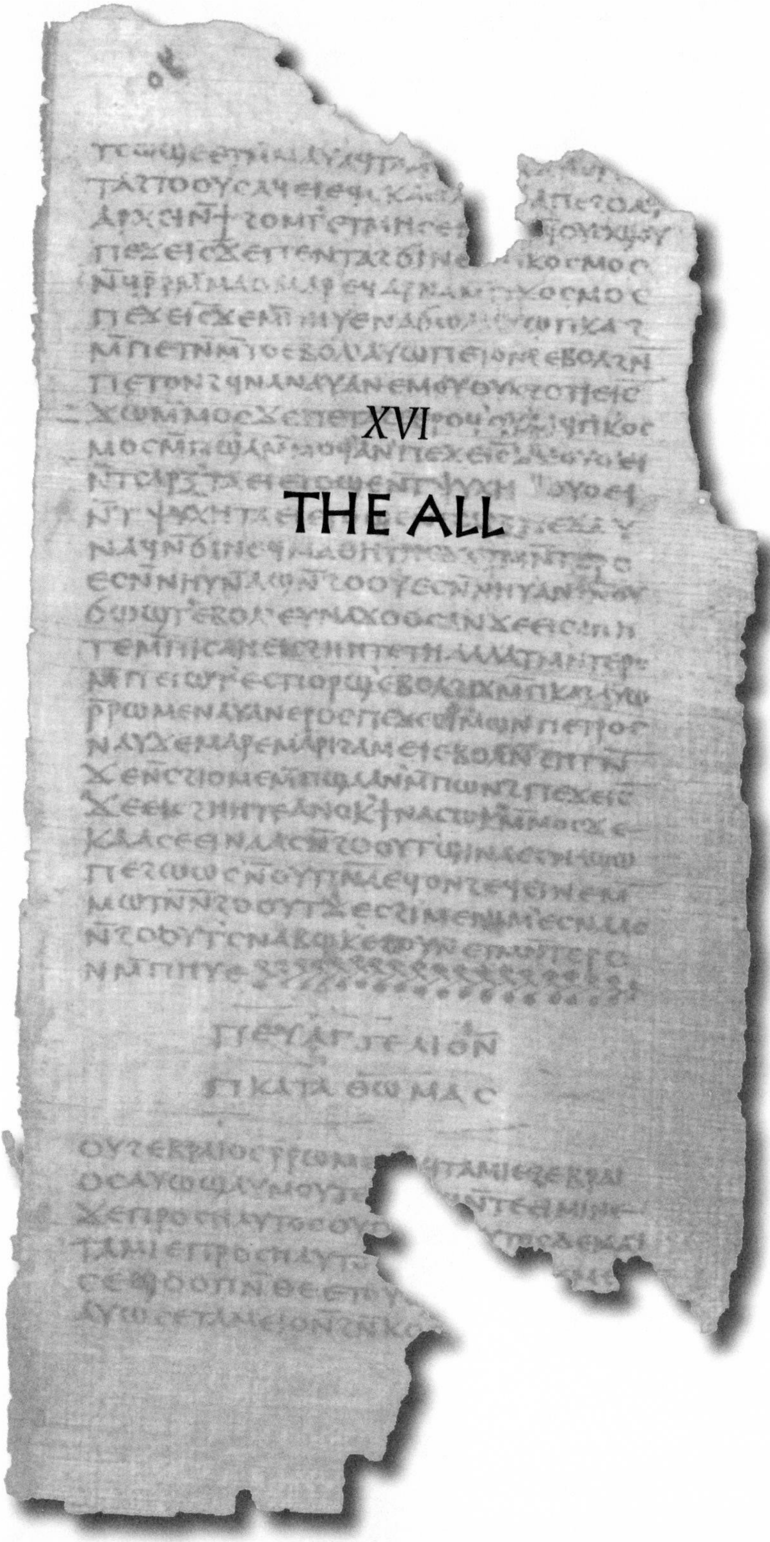

*When you see one
who was not born of woman,
bow down your face to the earth
and adore Him. He is your Father.*

(The Gospel of Thomas)

The Impenetrable and Indivisible is
He who exists
as God and Father of everything,
the Invisible One—above everything,
within which no corruption exists.
He is the pure light into which
no eye can look,

He is the invisible Spirit…
He does not exist in things
inferior to Him, since everything
exists in Him.

He is eternal…limitless…
unsearchable…immeasurable…
invisible…ineffable.
He is pure …Mind.

(The Apocryphon of John)

XVII

BECOMING ONE

*I came to make those things below
like the those things above,
and those things without
like those within.
I came to make them one.*

(The Gospel of Philip)

Whoever knows the Father
in pure knowledge
will depart to the Father
and rest in that
which has no beginning.

(*The Sophia of Jesus Christ*)

For when you leave the sufferings
and passions of the flesh behind,
you will receive rest from the Good One,
and you will reign with the King.
You will have joined with Him,
and He with you,
from then on,
for ever and ever.
Amen.

(The Book of Thomas the Contender)

Blessed is he who sees himself
as the fourth one
in Heaven.

(The Apocryphon of James)

XVIII

SUFFERING

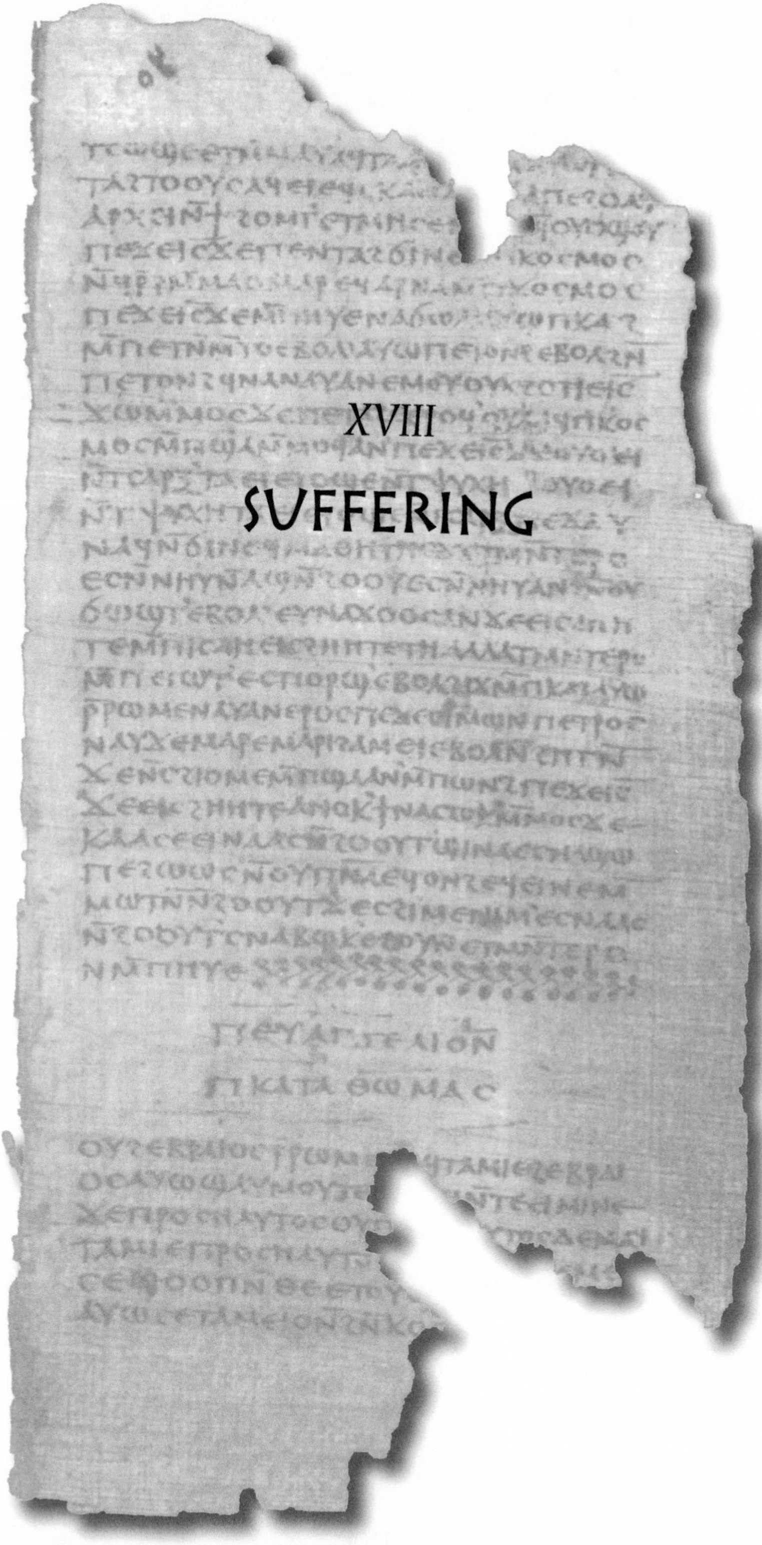

*They who would see Me
and reach my Kingdom
must attain Me
through pain and suffering.*

(*Agrapha*)

If you knew how to suffer
you would not be able to suffer.
Learn how to suffer and you
will overcome suffering.

(The Hymn of Jesus from the Acts of John)

Blessed are those who are
persecuted in their hearts.
They are those who
have known the Father in truth!

(The Gospel of Thomas)

Blessed are you when
you are hated and persecuted.
For your persecutors
will find no way
to pursue you...

(The Gospel of Thomas)

Blessed are you who are able to recognize
the stumbling blocks, and flee such things.
Blessed are you who are hated and not esteemed
because of the love your Lord has for you.
Blessed are you who weep and are
oppressed by those without hope,
for you will be released
from every bondage.

(The Book of Thomas the Contender)

James said to his brother, Jesus,
"Lord we obey you and have
left our fathers and our mothers
and our villages
and followed you.
Therefore, save us from
temptation by the evil one."

The Lord answered and said,
"How do you benefit if you
are not to be tempted, but overcome
through the grace of the Father?
But if you are lured by the evil one
and tormented by him—
and you still do God's will,
I tell you that He will love you,
and make you identical to Me.
You will become His beloved
through His grace,
and by your own choice.

(The Apocryphon of James)

198

So cease loving the body,
and do not fear suffering.
Why would you try to avoid suffering,
when the spirit surrounds you like a wall?
Think about how long
the world existed before you,
and will continue to exist after you.
You will discover that your life
is only a single day,
and your sufferings a single hour.

(The Apocryphon of James)

*When you come forth from
the sufferings and the passions
of the body, you will receive rest.*

(The Book of Thomas the Contender)

XIX

DEATH

When what animates
a person is removed,
that person is called dead,
and when what is alive
leaves what is dead,
that which is alive
will be called upon.

(Dialogue of the Savior)

Salome asked,
"How long will death rule?"
The Lord answered,
"As long as women continue
to bear children."

(The Gospel of the Egyptians)

The Disciples said to Jesus,
"Tell us how our end will come about."
Jesus said,
"Have you already found the beginning,
that you should ask about the end?
Blessed is that person
who reaches the beginning,
for he shall know the end.
And he will not experience death."

(The Gospel of Thomas)

His disciples said to him,
"On what day will rest come
to those who are dead,
and on what day
will the new world come?"
He said to them,
"The rest that you wait for
has already come,
and you have not recognized it."

(The Gospel of Thomas)

*Adam was produced by
a great power and a great wealth,
but he did not become worthy of you.
For had he been worthy, he would
not have experienced death.*

(The Gospel of Thomas)

*There are five trees for you
in Paradise which do not change
in summer and winter
and whose leaves do not fall.
Whoever knows them
will not taste death.*

(The Gospel of Thomas)

The heavens and the earth
will open in your presence.
And the one who lives in Him
will not see death.
He who becomes solitary
is superior to the world.

(The Gospel of Thomas)

Therefore seek out death,
like the dead who seek after life.
For that which is sought
will be revealed.
And the one who finds
will no longer be troubled.
When you come to understand death,
you will also understand salvation.
For I tell you this,
those who fear death cannot be saved;
for the Kingdom of God belongs
to those who put themselves to death.

(The Apocryphon of James)

Reject death, and think only of Life!
Remember my cross and my death,
and you will live.

(The Apocryphon of James)

Blessed is he who existed
before he came into being.

(The Gospel of Thomas)

XX

THE PASSION
OF THE CHRIST

He enlightened those
who were in darkness. . .
He brought Light to them and
showed them
the path of Truth to follow.

It was because of this that
Error became angry with Him,
persecuted Him, oppressed Him,
annihilated Him.

(The Gospel of Truth)

He abased himself even unto death
though clothed with immortal life.

(The Gospel of Truth)

For your sakes
I have placed myself
under a curse.

(The Apocryphon of James)

Understand, by dancing, what I do;
for yours is the Passion of Humanity
that I am to suffer.
Seeing what I suffer, you saw Me as suffering;
and seeing, you did not stand,
but were wholly moved—
moved to be wise.

(The Hymn of Jesus from The Acts of John)

"John, for the people below
in Jerusalem
I am being crucified
and pierced with spears
and whipped with reeds
and given vinegar
and bitter herbs to drink.
But to you I am speaking,
and listen to what I say . . ."

Then He showed me a Cross of Light. . .
and around the Cross was a great crowd,
which had no single form . . .

And I saw the Lord himself
above the Cross,
having no shape but only
a kind of voice;
yet not that voice which
we knew,
but one that was sweet
and gentle
and truly of God.

And he said,

"... *You hear that I suffered,*
yet I did not suffer;
and that I did not suffer,
yet I did suffer;
and that I was pierced,
yet I was not pierced;
that I was hanged,
yet I was not hanged;
that blood flowed from me,
yet it did not flow;
and that what they say
of me, I did not endure,
but what they do not say,
those things I did suffer.

Now what these are
I secretly show you;
for I know that you
will understand."

(*The Acts of John*)

213

He whom you see beside
the tree glad and laughing,
this is the Living Jesus.
But he into whose hands
and feet they drive the nails
is his fleshly likeness,
the ransom, which alone
they are able to put to shame.

(The Coptic Gnostic Apocalypse of Peter)

I am He who was within Me.
Never have I suffered in any way,
nor have I been distressed.
And this people
have done me no harm.

(The (first) Apocalypse of James)

THE FAREWELL

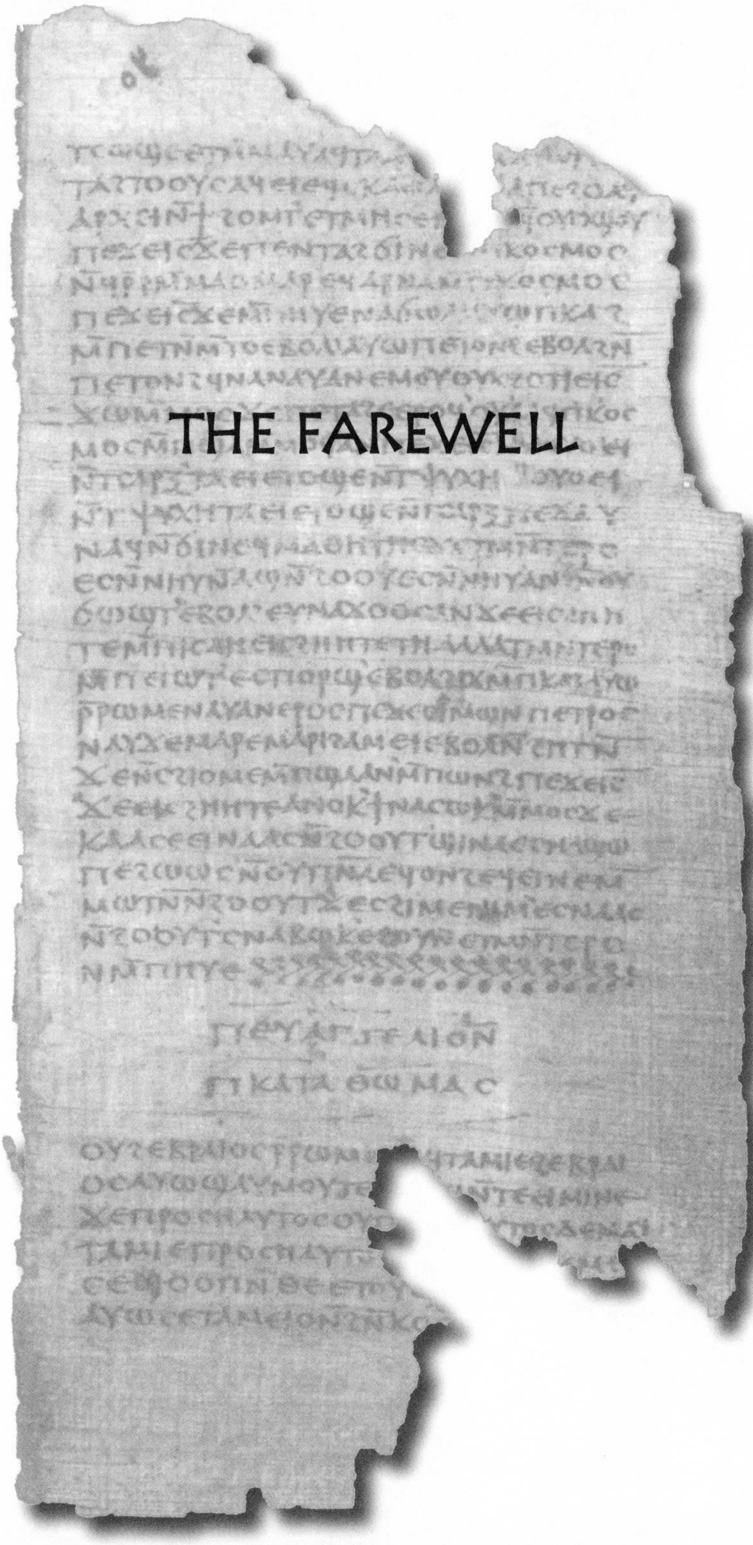

But give heed to the glory
that awaits me!
And when you have opened
your heart and turned it upwards,
listen to the hymns of the heavens!
For today I must take My place
at the right hand of the Father.
I have said My last word to you.
I shall separate from you.
For a chariot of spirit has
begun to bear me aloft.
And now I begin to unclothe myself,
that I may clothe myself.

(The Apocryphon of James)

Now, therefore,
follow me quickly.

(The Apocryphon of James)

Now go aboard the Ship of Light
and receive your garland of glory
and return to your kingdom
and rejoice with all the ages.

(The Living Gospel of Mani)

Lo, I am with you always.

Notes

[1] The earliest Christian Gospel, that of Mark's, was not written before 70 C.E. Like the other anonymous Gospel authors, the author of *Mark* was a Christian. Writing four decades after the death of Jesus—and probably from Rome—the author of *Mark* was not an eyewitness to the life and teachings of Jesus. As to the Christian Messiah and son of God, see notes 7—9 below.

[2] This is a subject still under debate, even among "liberal" New Testament scholars. An excellent presentation of the debate can be found in *The Apocalyptic Jesus—a Debate*; Dale Allison, Marcus Borg, John Dominic Crossan and Stephen Patterson, Santa Rosa, Polebridge Press, 2001.

[3] There are numerous "Introductions to the New Testament" which deal with this subject. One simple—and compassionate—primer I would recommend is *Meeting Jesus Again for the First Time* by Marcus Borg. For in depth studies: *The Birth of Christianity* by John Dominic Crossan, and *Introduction to the New Testament* by Raymond Brown.

[4] See also Robert Funk and the Jesus Seminar, *The Acts of Jesus*, San Francisco, HarperSanFrancisco, 1998.

[5] When I was in seminary thirty five years ago, the consensus then was that *Luke* was composed around 70 C.E. The date moved to the 90s some time later, and some scholars now believe *Luke* was written well into the second century. As with all dating of the Gospels, opinions—based on new research—continually change.

[6] See John S. Kloppenborg, Marvin W. Meyer, Stephen J. Patterson, Michael G. Steinhause, the *Q Thomas Reader*, Sonoma, Polebridge Press, 1990.

[7] Burton Mack, *A Myth of Innocence—Mark and Christian Origins*, Philadelphia, Fortress Press, 1991, p. 88.

[8] Burton Mack, *The Lost Gospel—The Book of Q & Christian Origins*, San Francisco, HarperSanFrancisco, 1993, pp. 73-80.

[9] Helmut Koester, *Ancient Christian Gospels*, Harrisburg, Penn., Trinity Press International, 1990, p. 86.

[10] See Gregory J. Riley, *One Jesus, Many Christs*, San Francisco, HarperSanFrancisco, 1989.

[11] In Karen King, *The Gospel of Mary of Magdala*, Santa Rosa, Polebridge Press, 2003, p. 6.

[12] Irenaeus, quoted in Elaine Pagels, *Beyond Belief, The Secret Gospel of Thomas*, New York, Random House, 2003, p. 159.

[13] Irenaeus, Ibid, p. 32

[14] Tertullian, c. 197 W) 3.249.

[15] Ibid, p. 177.

[16] Quoted in Time Magazine, December 22, 2003, p.61.

[17] Elaine Pagels, *Beyond Belief—The Secret Gospel of Thomas*, Random House, New York, 2003, p. 184.

[18] Ibid, p. 73.

[19] *The Gospel According to Mark* 4:11-12.

[20] C. H. Dodd, *Parables of the Kingdom*, London, Nisbet and Co, 1935, p. 16.

[21] Robert Eisenman, *James the Brother of Jesus*, New York, Penguin Books, 1997, p. 249

[22] See Morton Smith, *The Secret Gospel*, New York, Harper and Row, 1973

[23] This figure comes from The Jesus Seminar—a group of some one hundred scholars who spent fifteen years examining virtually every saying attributed to Jesus in the canonical Gospels. For a description of the process and the criteria used, see Robert J. Miller, *The Jesus Seminar and its Critics*, Sonoma, Polebridge Press, 1999. For those sayings of Jesus the Seminar considers authentic see, Robert W. Funk and The Jesus Seminar, *The Gospel of Jesus According to the Jesus Seminar*, Sonoma, Polebridge Press, 1999.

[24] *The Didache, Ancient Christian Writers*, Johannes Quasten and Joseph C. Plumpe, editors, New York, Paulist Press, 1948, p. 15.

[25] *Matthew* 7:13-14.

[26] C. H. Dodd, *Parables of the Kingdom*, New York, Charles Scribner's Sons, 1961, pp. 62f.

[27] *The Gospel of Thomas*, 113.

[28] Irenaeus (c. 280, E/W), 1.458, *A Dictionary of Early Christian Beliefs*, David W. Bercot, Editor, Peabody, Mass, 1998, p. 331.

[29] Tertullian (c. 197, W), 3.248m, Ibid, p. 333.

[30] Ibid, 3.249.

Sources

THE GOSPEL ACCORDING TO THOMAS

The Gospel According to Thomas is attributed to the disciple Thomas—or more accurately, Judas Thomas, who in this work is identified as the "twin" brother of Jesus: "These are the secret words that the living Jesus spoke and Didymus Judas Thomas wrote down." Didymus in Greek means "twin", as does Thomas in Aramaic. But Judas Thomas must be understood as the spiritual, not physical, twin of Jesus

Of all of the ancient Christian texts which have been (re)discovered over the past two centuries, *The Gospel According to Thomas* is by far the most important. What makes *Thomas* stand out above all other works is the fact that it contains a number of formerly "lost" sayings of the *historical* Jesus which are not found in any of the canonical Gospels. Secondly, *Thomas* contains sayings of Jesus that have parallels in the canonical Gospels, but the Thomasian versions of these sayings have been shown to be the more original versions.

Three fragments from *The Gospel of Thomas*—written in Greek—were discovered at Oxyrhynchus, Egypt, during the nineteenth century. But the entire text of *Thomas*—written in Coptic—was discovered at Nag Hammadi, Egypt, in 1945—and is part of the famous *Nag Hammadi Library*. The Oxyrhynchus papyruses have been dated to the third century C. E., while the Nag Hammadi papyrus dates to the fifth century. The original text of *Thomas*, however, was written during the first century C. E.

Thomas' 114 logia, or *sayings* of Jesus, were compiled in two stages. The first layer of *Thomas* was written around 50 C. E., making it one of the earliest known compilations of Jesus' teachings. A second, and clearly Gnostic, layer was added to *Thomas* sometime around the end of the first century. The *Gospel* is attributed to the disciple, Thomas, but like all early gospels, was composed anonymously.

THE BOOK OF THOMAS THE CONTENDER

Also discovered at Nag Hammadi, *The Book of Thomas the Contender* (or "spiritual athlete") is a revelation dialogue between the Christ—in a "revealed", non-physical, form—and his "twin", Judas Thomas. This document, along with *The Gospel of Thomas* and *The Acts of Thomas*, can be attributed to a Thomasian tradition which was primarily Gnostic-Christian. The work was probably composed sometime during the second half of the second century.

THE GOSPEL ACCORDING TO MARY (Magdalene)

The only Gospel attributed to a female disciple of Jesus, *The Gospel of Mary* was discovered in 1896—in the possession of an Egyptian antiquities dealer, and is part of a compilation of texts known as Codex Berolinensis 8502, or the *Berlin Codex*. This codex also contained three other works: *The Act of Peter*, *The Apocryphon of John*, and *The Sophia* (Wisdom) *of Jesus Christ*.

The Gospel of Mary is thought to have been produced in final form around 125 C. E., and is particularly important because it provides evidence of a struggle between matriarchal and patriarchal apostolic traditions in the early Church. Mary Magdalene's right to speak in Jesus' name in this text is challenged by Simon Peter and his brother, Andrew, who together represent the patriarchal viewpoint of orthodox Christianity. The Church, founded on the patriarchal traditions of Peter and Paul, found it necessary to suppress the tradition of Mary Magdalene, and deny her—and all women—the right to preach and teach in the Church.

Ten pages *of The Gospel According to Mary*—roughly half of the original work—are still missing.

THE ACTS OF JOHN

Even though it was considered heretical by the orthodox Church, *The Acts of John* has been handed down from ancient times through copying and recopying. *Acts* has some connection to Johannine literature in general, and may not have been in written before the third or fourth century. Many scholars, however, believe that the Hymn of Jesus—known also as the Round Dance of the Cross, and by other names—was part of a very early Christian ritual.

THE APOCRYPHON OF JOHN

A copy of the *Secret Book of John* was discovered at Nag Hammadi, but two other versions of John are also extant. This work, most likely written during the second half of the second century is clearly a Gnostic-Christian text, and has little relationship with other works attributed to the disciple, John.

THE BOOK OF JOHN THE EVANGELIST

Unknown prior to the twelve century, this text was probably written prior to the fourth century since it is clearly a Gnostic-Christian treatise that attributes creation to Satan, rather than to the Hebrew God, Yahweh. Its theology about the Christ is also docetic: Jesus was not human, but was of heavenly origin.

THE KERYGMATA PETROU

The *Kerygmata Petrou*, or "teachings of Peter" are actually part of a much larger work known as the *Pseudo-Clementines* (works "falsely" attributed to Clement of Rome, the early second century bishop of the Catholic Church.) The *Pseudo-Clementines* have not come down through history in their original form, but derive from a basic document thought to have been written during the middle of the third century. The text of the *Kerygmata*, like much of the *Pseudo-Clementines*, is largely Gnostic in origin, yet goes back to the core of Jewish-Christianity. Among other elements, it includes a very revealing polemic against the self-proclaimed apostle, Paul.

THE GOSPEL ACCORDING TO PHILIP

The *Gospel of Philip* was discovered at Nag Hammadi and is not a gospel in any true sense of the term. It contains only a few sayings attributed to Jesus, and is otherwise a theological exposition of the Valentinian school of Gnostic-Christianity. It was written as late as the second half of the third century.

THE APOCALYPSE OF PETER

The *Apocalypse of Peter* is another text that was discovered at Nag Hammadi, and was also written during the third century. It is a revelation dialogue between the "living" Jesus and Peter. The Apocalypse deals at some length with the persecution of Jesus, and the Gnostic-Christian understanding of his suffering. The anonymous author accuses the Church of being the true persecutor of the living Jesus.

THE APOCRYPHON OF JAMES

The Apocryphon, or Secret Book of James was discovered at Nag Hammadi in 1945. It takes the form of oral instructions given to Jesus' brother, James, and to Simon Peter, by the risen Christ during the 550 days that preceded his ascension. Probably written during the early part of the second century, Secret James shows Gnostic elements, but includes other early Christian material as well.

THE (FIRST) and (SECOND) APOCALYPSES OF JAMES

As with the Apocryphon of James, this text is attributed to James the Just. James was a Nazarite priest, the physical brother of Jesus, and leader of the early Jesus movement. Here, however, it is James' spiritual kinship with Jesus that is stressed. Both the first and second Apocalypses attributed to James were discovered at Nag Hammadi, thus both texts have Gnostic tendencies, while at the same time showing the influence of Jewish-Christianity. Both Apocalypses attributed to James compliment one another in stressing different aspects of the James tradition

THE GOSPEL OF THE HEBREWS; THE GOSPEL OF THE NAZOREANS AND THE GOSPEL OF THE EBIONITES

These three Gospels no longer exist, even in fragmentary form. They are known only through the testimony of early Church fathers who quoted from them. The names of the Gospels in those writings are often interchangeable, but scholars have determined that that the quotes come from three different Gospels. Because the Church patriarchs who quoted from these lost texts were the enemies of the Christians who used them, we cannot be sure that their quotes are accurate.

Each of these lost Gospels—like the canonicals—were narrative in style, and were probably written sometime during the first century. Jewish-Christianity—the earliest form of this faith—was eventually condemned as heresy by the orthodox Church.

THE DIDACHE (TEACHING OF THE TWELVE APOSTLES)

Mentioned in the writings of Clement of Alexandria, a single manuscript of *The Didache*, dated 1056, was discovered in 1873. The text itself was probably written during the second half of the first century. *The Didache* is an instruction manual for converts of an early Jewish-Christian community.

DIALOGUE OF THE SAVIOR

The single extant manuscript of *Dialogue* was discovered at Nag Hammadi in 1945. The dialogue is between the risen Christ and several of his disciples. *Dialogue* was probably composed during the first half of the second century, although parts of it may be earlier. Generally considered a "Gnostic" Gospel, *Dialogue* shares some similarities and comparisons with the *Gospel of Thomas*, the canonical Gospels of *John* and *Matthew*, and *The Apocryphon of James*.

THE GOSPEL OF EVE

The only Gospel under the name of an Old Testament figure, this lost Gospel of Gnostic character is mentioned only in the writings of Epiphanius, and the quote which appears in this work is the only known reference.

THE GOSPEL OF THE SAVIOR

This formerly lost Gospel was discovered in 1967 among the possessions of a Dutch antiquities dealer, and now resides in the Berlin Egyptian Museum. After many years of study by scholars, the text was published in 1997. The remains of this Gospel are extremely fragmentary, but enough of the text remains for scholars to be able to state that it is probably of Gnostic-Christian origin. While no date of composition has yet been determined, the manuscript was probably written no later than the beginning of the fourth century C. E.

THE EPISTULA APOSTOLORUM

Discovered in Cairo in 1895, and composed during the middle of the second century, the *Letter of the Apostles* is addressed to churches of "the four regions of the world". Its content is primarily orthodox—even anti-Gnostic at times—but still contains some Gnostic motifs. The *Epistula* can be credited to a form of Hellenized Egyptian-Jewish- Christianity.

THE (LIVING) GOSPEL OF MANI, THE MANICHEAN PSALMS
(Coptic Psalm Book), and THE BOOK OF MYSTERIES

These three works come from the third century school of Manichaeism founded by the prophet, Mani, and Mani himself may have written both the Gospel attributed to him, as well as *The Book of Mysteries*. A Persian mystic, the "arch-heretic" Mani fused Buddhism, Zoroastrianism and elements of Christianity to establish a new religion that was so popular, and so widespread, that it rivaled Catholic Christianity. Manichaeism may be considered a major world religion, and it existed in the East for centuries after it was suppressed in the West by the Church of Rome.

THE SOPHIA (WISDOM) OF JESUS CHRIST

Manuscripts of *The Sophia* were discovered both as part of the Berlin Codex, and again as part of *The Nag Hammadi Library*. A Gnostic revelation dialogue between the risen Christ and several of his disciples, the *Sophia* is a Christian reworking of a pagan text known as *Eugnostos the Blessed*, and may have been written as early as the second half of the first century.

THE PISTIS SOPHIA (Faith Wisdom)

A very lengthy revelation dialogue, the *Pistis Sophia* (Codex Askewianus) was discovered in a London bookstore in 1773. It consists of four sections or books. One section of the work is dated to the first half of the third century, while the other sections were composed later.

THE TWO BOOKS OF JEU

As part of *Codex Brucianus (Bruce Codex)*, *The Two Books of Jeu* (Jesus) was rediscovered in 1769, in Thebes, Egypt. It has much in common with *Codex Askewianus* and is mentioned twice in the *Pistis Sophia*. Composed during the first half of the third century, this work is another Gnostic-Christian revelation dialogue between the "living" Jesus and his disciples.

THE BOOK OF THE GREAT LOGOS ACCORDING TO THE MYSTERY

This title is the general heading for the manuscripts within the *Bruce Codex*—which contain *The Two Books of Jeu*.

THE GOSPEL OF TRUTH

A product of Valentinian Gnosticism, *The Gospel of Truth* was discovered at Nag Hammadi in 1945, and was referenced by the orthodox heresiologist, Irenaeus, in his *Adversus Haereses*. Composed during the middle of the second century, this work may have been written by Valentinus himself.

THE NAASSENE *PSALM OF THE SOUL*

The Naassenes were an early Gnostic-Christian "heretical" sect which the Church attacked through the writings of Irenaeus and Hippolytus. These heresiologists quoted from Naassene texts which are no longer extant. Our single quote comes from the writings of Hippolytus.

MANDAEAN LITURGY – from the *GINZA*

The Mandaeans, also known as Sabians, were generally thought to have founded their Gnostic sect prior to the formation of Christianity. Adherents claimed to be disciples of John the Baptist, and the sect itself has survived to the present day in Iran.

THE SECOND TREATISE OF THE GREAT SETH

Another revelation dialogue, this Gnostic-Christian work was discovered at Nag Hammadi. Purporting to give the true history of Jesus, and concentrating on his torture and crucifixion, this text maintains the docetic nature of Jesus' appearance on Earth.

General Source Text and Collections

New Testament Apocrypha, Volumes I & II, Wilhelm Schneemelcher, Editor, Revised Edition, Louisville, Westminster / John Knox Press, 1997.

The Apocryphal New Testament, M. R. James, Editor, London, Oxford University Press, 1976.

The Nag Hammadi Library, James M. Robinson, Editor, Revised edition, San Francisco, HarperSanFrancisco, 1990.

The Pistis Sophia—a Gnostic Gospel, G.R.S. Mead, Editor, USA, Garber Communications, 1984.

The Didache, Ancient Christian Writers, New York, Paulist Press, 1948.

Gospel of the Savior, Charles W. Hedrick, Paul A. Mirecki, Sonoma, Polebridge Press, 1999.

The Complete Gospels, Robert J. Miller, Editor, Sonoma, Polebridge Press, 1994.

For Further Study

Doresse, Jean, *The Secret Books of the Egyptian Gnostics*, New York, MJF Books, 1986.

Jonas, Hans, *The Gnostic Religion*, Boston, Beacon Hill, 1958.

King, Karen, *What Is Gnosticism?* Cambridge, Harvard University Press, 2003.

Koester, Helmut, *Ancient Christian Gospels*, Harrisburg, Trinity Press International, 1990.

Mead, G.R.S., *Fragments of a Faith Forgotten*, London, Theological Publishing Society, 1906.

Pagels, Elaine, *The Gnostic Gospels*, New York, Random House, 1979.

About the author

Richard Hooper received his Bachelor of Arts degree in the Philosophy of Religion from San Francisco State University in 1966, and his Master of Divinity degree from Pacific Lutheran Theological Seminary in 1970. He was ordained by the American Lutheran Church in 1971, and for the following eight years conducted a specialized ministry to the counter culture on the Monterey Peninsula in California. In 1978, Richard left the ministry to become a nature recordist and radio commentator. He subsequently founded the Nature Recordings© and World Disc Music© record labels, and was CEO of World Disc Productions© for many years. Throughout his business career, the author has maintained his interest in the continuing "quest for the historical Jesus", and his studies in the field of Gnostic-Christianity and the early Church. As a lay scholar, Richard Hooper is an associate member of the Jesus Seminar, and weekly columnist on religion and spirituality for United Press International (UPI). Share his weekly insights at: www.ReligionAndSpiritualityForum.com

Also available by Richard Hooper:

The Crucifixion of Mary Magdalene:
The Historical Tradition of the First Apostle,
and the Ancient Church's Campaign to Suppress It

Visit our website at: www.SanctuaryPublications.com

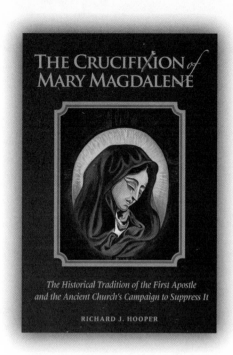

THE CRUCIFIXION *of* MARY MAGDALENE

The Historical Tradition of the First Apostle and the Ancient Church's Campaign to Suppress It

RICHARD J. HOOPER

From the earliest days of Christianity, Mary Magdalene has been the subject of controversy, rumor and innuendo. Yet the historical Mary was neither a prostitute nor the wife of Jesus. The canonical Gospels are clear that Mary was Jesus' most faithful disciple. She remained to witness his crucifixion after all of the male disciples had fled in fear. Shortly after Jesus died, she had a powerful experience of the living Jesus and, as a consequence, became the first apostle of Christianity. The Gnostic Gospels further claim that Mary was a leader, teacher, visionary, and—because of her holiness—Jesus' most beloved disciple.

And yet the early Church felt threatened by Mary Magdalene to such an extent that it found it necessary to obscure her real importance, alter her historical tradition, suppress the theology she became associated with, and ultimately discredit her by reinventing her as a wanton woman.

Through a careful examination of more than twenty ancient texts in which Mary Magdalene appears, the author—a former Lutheran pastor—lays bare orthodox Christianity's age-old conspiracy against Mary, and reveals her true role as the primary founder of Christian faith.

350 pages • ISBN 0974699543 • 9780974699554 • $19.95

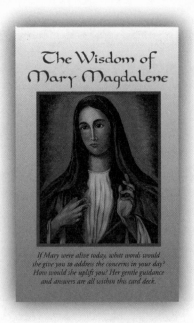

ALSO AVAILABLE FROM
SANCTUARY PUBLICATIONS:

The Wisdom of Mary Magdalene
Meditational Card Deck

Created by Sharon Hooper

With illustrations by Susun Lovit

www.SanctuaryPublications.com

info@SanctuaryPublications.com

Featuring 36 Gospel quotations and richly colored artistic
masterpieces depicting the life and wisdom of Jesus and Mary
Magdalene. Includes a 90-page guidebook providing layouts and
offering uplifting, practical advice that bridges the teachings of
Mary and Jesus with the life questions you face today.

For further information, please contact:

Sanctuary Publications
P. O. Box 20697
Sedona, AZ 86341
info@SanctuaryPublications.com